11 Ramah Bay	**16** Angkor Wat	**21** Manchester	**26** Sumer
12 Rapa Nui	**17** Cape of Good Hope	**22** Mecca	**27** Taj Mahal
13 Teotihuacán	**18** Giza	**23** Petra	**28** Thebes & Valley of the Kings
14 Tenochtitlán	**19** Great Wall of China	**24** Pompeii	**29** Venice
15 Tikal	**20** Great Zimbabwe	**25** Seville	**30** Xianyang

From *THEN* to **NOW**

A SHORT HISTORY OF THE WORLD

CHRISTOPHER MOORE

Illustrated by ANDREJ KRYSTOFORSKI

TUNDRA BOOKS

For Suz and Jon
— A.K.

Text copyright © 2011 by Christopher Moore Editorial Ltd.
Illustrations copyright © 2011 by Andrej Krystoforski

Published in Canada by Tundra Books,
75 Sherbourne Street, Toronto, Ontario M5A 2P9

Published in the United States by Tundra Books of Northern New York,
P.O. Box 1030, Plattsburgh, New York 12901

Library of Congress Control Number: 2010927033

Library and Archives Canada Cataloguing in Publication

Moore, Christopher, 1950-
From then to now : a short history of the world / Christopher Moore
(author) ; Andrej Krystoforski (illustrator).

Includes index.
ISBN 978-0-88776-540-7

1. World history – Juvenile literature. 2. Civilization – History – Juvenile
literature. I. Krystoforski, Andrej, 1943- II. Title.

D20.M76 2011   j909   C2010-902852-X

We acknowledge the financial support of the Government of Canada through the Book Publishing Industry Development Program (BPIDP)
and that of the Government of Ontario through the Ontario Media Development Corporation's Ontario Book Initiative.
We further acknowledge the support of the Canada Council for the Arts and the Ontario Arts Council for our publishing program.

ONTARIO ARTS COUNCIL
CONSEIL DES ARTS DE L'ONTARIO

Map endpapers: The maps are not comprehensive, but serve only as a guide to the places named in the text.

Original portrait of Queen Victoria: Hutton Archive | Stringer | Getty Images

Medium: watercolor and gouache on paper

Design: Jennifer Lum

Printed and bound in China

1 2 3 4 5 6   16 15 14 13 12 11

CONTENTS

Author's Note   iv

Preface   1

1   Hunters and Gatherers   3

2   Learning to Farm   21

3   The Golden Empires: 5000 BCE — 1000 CE   35

4   Gods and Lawgivers: 5000 BCE — 1000 CE   53

5   The Greeks and Romans: 500 BCE — 500 CE   63

6   A Peninsula West of Asia   77

7   Explorers and Colonies   93

8   The Age of Industry   115

9   Europe's World   133

10   The Stormy Twentieth Century   153

Epilogue: The Global City   181

Index   185

Author's Note

Dates in this book are written as BCE (Before the Common Era) or CE (Common Era). Europeans used to count the years as BC (Before Christ) or AD (*Anno Domini* in Latin, meaning "in the Year of the Lord"). Most of the world now uses the same dates, but with BCE and the CE in place of the specifically Christian terms.

PREFACE

When does a history of the world – even a short history of the world – start?

This history starts with people. This is not a book about the formation of the planet billions of years ago, or the life and death of the dinosaurs millions of years ago. It follows the story of our species, humanity – what scientists call Homo sapiens, "thinking humans." It's about what we know of people like us, on our planet, throughout time. It starts about fifty thousand years ago.

CHAPTER ONE

HUNTERS *and* GATHERERS

D id you ever go farther than a car or motorboat could take you, to a place where you could see no lights, no roads? To a place where no phones rang, beyond the view of power lines and buildings, beyond the rumble of traffic? At night you saw no city lights glowing on the horizon, but a billion stars blazed fiercely overhead. Outside the crackling comfort of your fire there was only darkness, with the rustle of insects and an animal's distant cry. You could feel for a moment that you and your companions might be the only people on the face of the earth.

Until about ten thousand years ago, humans didn't know how to farm. They survived by hunting wild animals and gathering wild plants.

3

Hardly any of us go to such places today. These places are hard to find. There are telephones in the jungle, and ski huts on the glaciers. Gum wrappers and cola cans litter the slopes of Mount Everest and the shores of the most remote islands. Even the parks and preserved areas where we go to experience wild nature are hemmed in by the world that we ourselves have shaped.

Once, the whole world was the wild, natural place you sensed by that lonely campfire. People followed animal trails out of the forest, walked through tall waving grass forever, followed a tumbling clear river down to great waters. The air was alive with birds large and small, in flocks that darkened the sky. Herds of animals grazed across the grasslands to the horizon. Every bush and patch of brush sang with insects. People left hardly a trace of themselves on the landscape – no buildings, no fences, no farms or towns or cleared fields, only a few pathways. The earth was nature's planet.

4

That time was not so very long ago. Our planet is more than four billion years old. Dinosaurs roamed it a hundred million years ago. Compared to that, the time of our human species is barely more than the blink of an eye. Sixty thousand years, say. A hundred thousand years, tops. If the time since the dinosaurs were the length of a movie, the time of humans would be shorter than the credits at the movie's end.

Our Human Species

Human time starts in Africa. That continent was the home of our most distant ancestors, five million years ago or more. More than a million years ago, some branches of the human family (scientists call them "hominids" because they are humanlike but not really human) spread out from Africa. These hominids lived in the Middle East, in Europe, and in Asia for hundreds of thousands of years. But those branches of the humanlike family died off, and left no descendants. Modern humans came along more recently, barely a hundred thousand years ago, and they too developed in Africa. All the people in the world today are descended from them.

These people, Homo sapiens, could reason and speak and sing and plan as well as we can. They could use fire and make clothes and tools. These were people we could recognize as our own species. They were like us.

Peopling the Planet

Homo sapiens, our species, spread out into the world during an ice age, during tens of thousands of years of bad weather, when ice covered much of the planet. So much water was locked up in ice that sea levels were much lower than they are today. Icebergs from the frozen polar seas chilled the oceans that remained. Sixty thousand years ago, the world was cold and getting colder. Even the high places – the Himalayas of Asia, the Alps of Europe, the Rockies and Andes of the Americas, the Snowy Mountains of Australia – lay deep under ice that slowly flowed out into surrounding lowlands. These creeping rivers of ice – glaciers – rumbled down out of the Arctic to cover half of North America and much of northern Europe and northern Asia. Even at the equator, glaciers flowed down from high peaks. The last trace of Africa's ice age, the shrinking snowcap of Mount Kilimanjaro in Africa, is still melting away. And Africa was not only cooler then but drier, with grasslands or deserts where lush rainforests stand today.

There is a place in southern Africa where archeologists have found shells pierced with holes, ready for stringing on a thread. Those shells are 75,000 years old, and someone made them into jewelry. Way back then, people's hands could use tools, and their minds could imagine beauty. About the time those beads were made, some of those people began to move out of Africa and into neighboring continents. Were they pushed by population growth, or by changing climates, or pulled by the need to explore? Whatever the reason, those people were Homo sapiens, like us, and they were ready to discover the world.

The total human population was small then, and people didn't leave much behind them — they didn't build cities or roads — so it's hard to trace their route. But we know that these ancestors of ours traveled far. Fifty thousand years ago, they had spread into the Middle East as well as most of Africa. Some had moved north and west toward Europe. They had gone to India, begun to settle in China, and moved down through Southeast Asia to voyage by raft across broad stretches of water to reach New Guinea, Australia, and Tasmania, which were all combined in one continent at that time.

About twenty thousand years ago, increased sunshine began to warm earth's people. This was not because of anything people did. It was part of a long cycle in our planet's orbit around the sun and the way the earth tilts on its axis. The earth warmed, the great glaciers began to melt and shrink, and the oceans rose higher as water from the melting glaciers poured into them. As the world grew less cold, humans explored more of it.

Even in the worst days of the age of ice, people had lived on the steppes (plains) of Ukraine and Central Asia, almost within sight of the glaciers. Wrapping themselves in carefully stitched fur-lined clothing, they had warmed their dwellings, built of bone and hide, with lamps that burned animal fat. They had transported meat and goods on sleds they could haul smoothly across the snowy landscape. They were experts on survival.

Now, as the glaciers retreated from central Europe, from northern Russia and Siberia, and from high mountain ranges everywhere, people boldly moved even farther from the African lands where humans had begun. Equipped only with fire and clothing, and with the skills they carried in their brains and shared through the gift of language, humans adapted to new places and different climates. They found landmarks and sacred places wherever they went. They learned what plants they could gather and what animals they could hunt on each new hillside, in each new river valley, that they discovered.

Humans reached Siberia as far back as fifteen thousand years ago. It was possible to walk from Siberia into Alaska then, because the sea level was still low and no strait separated Asia from North America. But how people came to the Americas is still one of the most mysterious parts of our early history. Although Siberia and Alaska were joined, huge glaciers blocked the route from Alaska to the rest of the Americas. Because of that, archeologists used to assume that humans could not have made that trip until the glaciers melted, about fourteen thousand years ago. Yet today archeologists are sure they have found evidence of human settlements older than that, far down toward the southern tip of South America. How did people reach the bottom of South America if glaciers still blocked their way across northwestern Canada?

Right now, no one knows for sure. Could people from northeast Asia have moved into North America *before* glaciers blocked the routes, as far back as thirty thousand years ago, even before people settled in Siberia? Probably not. It's more likely that the first people who moved from Siberia into Alaska continued to travel, perhaps in small boats, down the northwest coast of North America. At the time, that coast looked the way Greenland does today; it was ringed with mighty ice walls, yet rich with fish and seals and all the bounty of northern oceans. If those daring wanderers ventured down the coast to a place south of the glaciers, they could have come ashore, learned to live in this new land, and spread across North America, and South America too, as the climate grew warmer. It seems that these were the ancestors of the many First Nations of the Americas. It still mystifies us how they managed to make these continents their home, and this should make us respect them even more.

After humans moved into the Americas, only one large part of the world remained uninhabited: the islands of the Pacific Ocean. About five thousand years ago, people from Taiwan, China, and the islands of Southeast Asia were already masters of seamanship and ocean navigation. They began exploring eastward, across the nets of islands leading into the center of the Pacific.

Here was a bold adventure. The Pacific Islanders launched themselves into the vast ocean in sailing canoes carved from a single log, with "outrigger" arms on either side to help them balance in heavy waves. Carrying stone tools, a few seeds and plants, and pigs and chickens, they ventured far out of sight of land. Spreading through the South Pacific, they settled even very isolated islands.

These sailors of the Pacific settled Fiji almost three thousand years ago, and Samoa, Tahiti, and other island groups in the next few hundred years. Fifteen hundred years ago, they reached the Hawaiian Islands, far

THE *MOAIS* OF RAPA NUI

As people migrated, they took with them their sacred beliefs and rituals. On the small island of Rapa Nui, 2,200 miles (3,540 kilometers) from South America, stand hundreds of mysterious figures called *moais*. They are carved from volcanic rock, and some are as tall as a four-story building. Who were the artists? They may have sailed here from Polynesia in giant canoes, and they likely set up the statues as idols or memorials. But their story has been lost, and only these strange, brooding monuments remain.

to the north, and Rapa Nui (Easter Island), over toward South America. Surely these were the greatest sailors of ancient times. They became known as Polynesians, from words meaning "many islands."

One of the last large habitable island areas to become home to humans was New Zealand. Just about a thousand years ago, a few shiploads of explorers came ashore on a coast no human being had seen before. They stayed on the lush green islands and developed the Maori civilization — some forty thousand years after neighboring Australia had received its first human settlers.

Ice-Age Hunters

Cast your light on the wall. Animals leap out at you: reindeer, horses, bulls, even thick-maned lions and curved-tusked mammoths. They charge, they run, they leap. Some are surrounded by arrows or spears. Sometimes a hunter has placed his handprint among them. You are deep in a cave in the mountain, it is the Ice Age, and you could be anywhere across southern Europe, from Spain deep into Russia.

During the era of icy cold, maybe thirty thousand years ago, people in Europe and western Asia had begun to paint animals on cave walls. It was a grim, difficult time. The hill country along the Mediterranean coast of France and Spain was a frigid, treeless tundra not far from glaciers that grew thicker every winter and rumbled relentlessly southward. Small numbers of people whose ancestors had come in better times endured there, living in igloo-like shelters with walls built from the scavenged bones of mammoths. Reindeer in great herds migrated across this landscape, and the people hunted them as they passed. To survive, these hunting bands had to share knowledge about the herds and their movements, so they would meet and plan as one people. In the places where they gathered, they painted – to honor the spirits of the animals, to teach hunting skills to their young, perhaps simply to celebrate skill and artistry. Sharing, communicating, exchanging precious knowledge about animals and the hunt: these activities helped humankind survive. Lavishing their talents on painted visions of animals on the walls of caves was part of the ritual.

When the world began to grow warmer, about fifteen thousand years ago, the tundra of Europe and western Asia slowly became forests and grasslands. Food from both animals and plants became more abundant. Instead of hunting reindeer, people pursued deer, wild pigs, and other forest creatures. Human populations grew larger and were not so closely bound together. They no longer gathered to plan how to ambush the reindeer herds.

When the reindeer hunters' gatherings ceased, so did their cave paintings. These hunters were not the only artists in the world; spectacular rock art had appeared from southern Africa to Australia. But the reindeer hunters' painting tradition had lasted a very long time – twenty thousand years, two hundred centuries – before it gave way to other skills and other arts. All over Europe, caves lined with these ancient treasures were abandoned and allowed to fill with debris. These spectacular art galleries that had helped early people survive ice-age conditions would not be seen again until they were rediscovered in the 1900s.

The Changing Earth

As the Ice Age ended, water from the melting glaciers began to pour into the oceans. Sea levels all over the world rose by at least 330 feet (100 meters). Many fertile coastal places that had been home to early humans vanished deep under the water. The lowlands around the Mediterranean Sea were drowned. So were the northwest American coasts that may have been humanity's route into the Americas. The North Sea flooded a great plain that had once linked Britain to Europe and Scandinavia. The lowlands of Southeast Asia were submerged and the highlands became islands and peninsulas. Tasmania, which had been settled by humans while it was joined to Australia, became an island. For ten thousand years the people who lived there were cut off from Australia by a wide, stormy ocean strait.

Not only the shorelines were altered. The ecology of every continent went through rapid change as the cold, dry Ice Age gave way to warmer, wetter times. We cannot follow all the steps by which tundra in the north became plains and then forest, or how African deserts became grassy savannas, open forests, and eventually deep jungle. But we know that, where the sands of the Sahara desert now blow, people once lived by lakes and rivers. The deep jungles of Southeast Asia were once temperate (mild) forest environments. Reindeer, once at home on the tundra of the south of France, slowly followed the ice back toward northern Europe, and then into the far north of Scandinavia and Russia. Many plant species had been destroyed in the north by the Ice Age, and plant life had to spread back from zones of refuge farther south.

Our human species struggled to adapt to these radical changes, but many animal species died out. When people had first come into the

Americas, they had encountered elephants, or at least mammoths and mastodons, the hairy, curved-tusked relatives of elephants. Everywhere they went, in Europe, Asia, the Americas, and Australia, they had lived with Ice Age animals much different from those we know today. The American continents had beavers the size of bears and huge meat-eating birds called teratorns, as well as saber-toothed wildcats and camels. Australia had a giant kangaroo and a kind of lion. The plains and forests of Europe were prowled by woolly rhinoceroses and giant elk.

During the great climate change and the worldwide expansion of the human population, many of the large animal species in Europe and Australia plunged into extinction, and three-quarters of those in the Americas disappeared. This was partly because of the warming; species that had adapted to the cold tundra and forest or to dry semi-deserts died away as their habitats changed dramatically. But in many parts of the world, the hard-pressed animals encountered another threat: human hunters. The Ice Age creatures of northern Europe, Australia, and the Americas died out just about the time people suddenly invaded their homelands.

Were early people mighty hunters, that they could drive so many species to extinction? Probably not. In Africa, people and animals had lived together for a long time, and most species of large animals, including the rhinos, elephants, giraffes, and hippopotamuses we know today, survived the hunters as well as the changing climate. In Australia, the first humans arrived long before the rapid change in the climate, and they co-existed with giant kangaroos and enormous wombats until rapid warming about ten thousand years ago destroyed the conditions in which these animals thrived. Even in North America, where people arrived and animals vanished at about the same time, the changing climate probably did more than human hunters to doom the Ice Age species. Across the Americas, archeologists have found the bones of mammoths and other extinct species with spear points in them, but the changed climate was still probably the main reason they were driven to extinction. Yet other species made the transition to a warmer world quite successfully. During the Ice Age, bison lived in the forests of North America, but they adapted to the change in weather and soon ranged the new grasslands in vast herds.

By the time the climate settled into the pattern it has had for most of the last ten thousand years, Homo sapiens had populated most of the world. With the climate so much milder, with plant and animal species spreading into once-icebound regions, the human population was probably growing rapidly for the first time since the Ice Age had laid its cold hands on the world.

And like the climate and the plants and the animals, human beings changed as they learned to live in a changed world.

How Hunter-Gatherers Lived

For nine-tenths of the span of human history, we have survived as hunters and gatherers. In a few places, people still do. Hunter-gatherers are people who do not grow crops or raise livestock. They rarely build shelters to last much more than a season. They do not use metals or pottery. They live by simply hunting and gathering food.

Hunter-gatherers live lightly upon the land but they need a lot of space in which to hunt and forage (gather food). Later farming peoples sometimes imagined that their ancestors who hunted were simply homeless wanderers. Really, hunters and gatherers thrived by knowing every detail of the landscape in which they lived: where flints and obsidian (glass from volcanoes) for tools could be found, what regions were most fertile in summer and which offered shelter in winter, where animals could be found at each season of the year, exactly when each kind of plant and root and seed came into ripeness, when and where fish migrated up the rivers to spawn.

Hunter-gatherers always needed to know what was over the next mountain range, or beyond the unwelcoming dry lands. Indeed, that alone may explain why they spread out to populate the world. But people who lived by hunting and gathering were also very local. They prospered by knowing their own terrain and its plants and animals and sacred places. As our species spread out to create a whole world of human settlement, we also became tens of thousands of separate bands and families and communities, each at home in its own place, with its own language, its own beliefs, and its own way of living. All these groups were descended from the same African ancestors, but they had grown unaware of each other, working out their own destiny in their own way.

Over many years, as these separate groups grew in population and adapted to their different environments, they began to look different. As the differences were passed down the generations, inherited by children from their parents, they became more obvious. Asians began to look quite different from East Africans, East Africans from native Americans, native Americans from Northern Europeans, Northern Europeans from South Asians, South Asians from West Africans, and so on. Many of these differences may have been largely accidental; if a few ancestors had a certain eye-fold or hair color, or even a shape of big toe, it might become common among their descendants. Other differences were useful adaptations. Pale skin and fair hair were helpful in northern climates where the skin had to absorb as much sunshine as possible. Darker skin was a protection against the fierce sun of tropical regions.

THE CAMEL-LEOPARD GIRAFFE

People in prehistoric times respected the animals they hunted. One that was much admired in Africa was the giraffe, the world's tallest living animal, which can grow as tall as eighteen feet (over five meters). Giraffe images appear in prehistoric cave paintings, and early writings marvel at their height. Giraffes were considered symbols of rain, prosperity, fertility, and strength, and in later years they were sent as diplomatic gifts to rulers of places that didn't have them. The modern name, "giraffe," comes from the Arabic term *zarafah*; giraffes used to be called "camelopards," because they were shaped a bit like camels, and spotted sort of like leopards.

The simplicity of hunter-gatherer life might shock or even terrify us. We find it difficult to imagine ourselves living our whole lives outdoors, with only the goods we can carry, and only a cave or skin tent to shelter us. But hunting and gathering people have rarely been eager to give up their way of life. For them, the way to live well is to live with little. Most hunting-gathering peoples were strong and flourishing and ate a healthy diet. They rarely worked as hard or as long as farmers or city-dwellers, and because they shared their life and their work, they had more equality than many other societies.

Hunter-gatherers were deeply linked to the natural world. They moved with the seasons, enjoyed the bounty of good times, and expected little protection against bad times. If their food plants withered for lack of water and the animals they hunted grew scarce, the people had to move on or die. They viewed the spirit world as part of that natural world. Because they depended on animals, they believed that they shared the world with animal spirits. They did not own the animals they hunted, any more than they owned the land or the plants growing on the land. They felt that they had to respect and honor the animals, so that the animals would give themselves to humans as food.

THE ALL-GIVING BUFFALO

The American buffalo (more correctly called "bison") was essential for many native peoples in North America. Buffalo meat was a favorite food, pelts provided warm clothing and shelter, and bones were made into tools. It's no wonder the buffalo was seen as a symbol of abundance and sacred life, a spirit being who gave people everything they needed. Buffaloes appear in native stories, their skulls were used in rituals, and an entire head was sometimes worn as a mask in a traditional dance.

That hunter-gatherer sense of equality within the natural world shaped the way early humans related to each other. Most people spent the majority of their lives in small bands or family groups. Men and women who were strong or skillful or wise or persuasive earned respect, and became leaders and shamans (priests). But no one was either rich or poor, and no powerful class ruled over the others. Hunter-gatherer life could not support complexities like royal families or nobles or special luxuries. The hunters and gatherers who first went out and settled the earth were as wise as us, as clever, and as creative. It may seem odd to accept that they had no writing or reading, almost no pottery, no metal, no fabrics, and few possessions. But these were the people who populated our planet. This is the way most people lived for most of the history of Homo sapiens.

History, the kind of history that has people's names and written stories, and nations and kings, and endless changes and developments, and children who live lives quite different from the lives of their parents – hunter-gatherers might say that all this is new and peculiar, and not a normal way for people to live.

Traders

On the north coast of Labrador, in Canada, where the five-thousand-foot (1,500-meter) peaks of the Torngat Mountains plunge into the iceberg-choked North Atlantic, there is an inlet called Ramah Bay. Along the shore of Ramah Bay lies an outcropping of a glasslike, milky-colored mineral called "chert." Up and down the coast there is nothing else like it; you can almost see through a chip of Ramah chert. It is beautiful, and it is useful, too. A skilled stonecutter can fracture chert to form tools with razor-sharp edges: knives, axes, spear points, scythes. These are tools that keep a hunting-gathering people alive.

BOWHEAD WHALE

Native communities in the Arctic depended on the bowhead whale for thousands of years, much as natives farther south depended on the buffalo. The whale supplied food, tools, and building materials. Strips of its baleen – the strong, elastic "strainer" in the whale's mouth, used to catch tiny plankton – were used to make baskets and art. The whale hunt was necessary but sacred; hunters performed special ceremonies when they killed a whale, so the animal's spirit would not be offended.

No one lives at bleak, cold, treeless Ramah Bay, but for six thousand years people were drawn to that rugged place to gather chert. For thousands of years, they traded this precious commodity across networks that stretched far across what is now northern Canada, and down the Atlantic coast of what is today the United States.

Glassy chert from Ramah Bay was just one of many valuable objects traded among hunters and gatherers for thousands of years: ivory in Africa, glassy black volcanic obsidian in the hills of Turkey, exotic feathers from the mountains of New Guinea, glittering seashells from the Australian coasts, nuggets of gold in the Andes mountains of South America. When hunting peoples met, they traded goods and hunting news. They might even exchange sons and daughters, to build new families and forge alliances among neighbors. Humanity is a trading species, really the only species that trades. Trading, even the simple trades that took our ancestors to cold, remote places like Ramah Bay, was a crucial part of what enabled humans to make the immense transition from hunting to farming.

CHAPTER TWO

LEARNING *to* FARM

Becoming farmers was one of the greatest changes our human species has ever made, and one of the most difficult. How did hunter-gatherers who lived in a world of wild plants and animals, taking a little of what they needed, settle down to own land, to plow fields, to raise herds of animals? How did people in the Chang (Yangtze) valley of China somehow manage to transform an ordinary wetland plant called *oryza* into rice, over many thousands of years? How did people in Mexico turn an insignificant wild grass into the plant we know today as corn or maize? Let's visit some of the world's first farmers, and see what they did.

The ancient Scythians were nomads who more or less lived on horseback. They may have been the first people to tame horses and ride them. They also made intricate gold jewelry.

Gardeners of the Middle East

Almost twelve thousand years ago, when a sudden brief spurt of global warming marked the end of the hundred-thousand-year age of ice, the land east of the Mediterranean Sea became a lush environment of oak forests and grassy slopes, its valleys dotted with lakes, its plains flooded by broad rivers. This land was now a hunter-gatherer's paradise. People could collect acorns and almonds, as well as berries, fruit, and honey, for much of the year. They could harvest plants, roots, and seeds, and also the many grubs and other insects that lived in the vegetation. This rich country-side supported endless herds of gazelles and other animals, and there were fish and shellfish in the rivers, the lakes, and the Mediterranean.

WITCHETTY GRUBS

In some places, bugs are still a popular dish. The Aboriginal people of Australia have learned to live in the hot, dry interior, where food is scarce. One of their favorite snacks is witchetty grubs — white, finger-sized larvae of moths and beetles that they dig out of the trunks and roots of trees. The grubs can be eaten alive, or baked in the hot ashes of a fire, or roasted like marshmallows. According to one description, they taste like scrambled eggs with peanut butter.

By 10,000 BCE, some of the hunter-gatherers of these Middle Eastern lands lived so well that they did not have to keep migrating from place to place, as most hunter-gatherers always had. They had so many animals to hunt nearby, and so many plants to gather, that families or bands could settle in one place for much of the year. They were not yet farmers but they were almost gardeners, using stone-bladed sickles to gather wild grains to store in woven baskets or leather bags. They seem to have been among the first humans to domesticate dogs. They may even have begun to keep other animals for meat or milk. Since they no longer had to carry everything with them on a constant round of migrations, they could build permanent homes and other buildings, own more possessions, and store nuts and seeds out of season. With their new prosperity, they could even begin to support people who practiced special skills and crafts.

Wild gardens like these existed in other parts of the world too: on the island of New Guinea, in the river valleys of China, in Central American valleys, in parts of Africa. Here and there, some hunting and gathering peoples began to stop migrating. They were still hunting wild game and gathering wild plants, but they settled in one place. They built homes that became villages. Around these quiet villages, history began to speed up.

Wheat — the Staff of Life

In these garden-like paradises that flourished in the Middle East ten thousand years ago, wild cereal plants thrived. These were the ancestors of wheat, rye, barley, and other crops we grow today. For many centuries, people in the Middle East gathered these wild grains each summer as they ripened, just the way they gathered wild fruits, nuts, roots, and other plants.

There is one great difference between wild plants and "domesticated" plants. Wild grains spill their seeds naturally, and the seeds fall to the ground and grow into the next crop. But domesticated plants need someone to harvest them. They need human assistance, and they would not survive without it. Pods of wild peas split open when the peas inside grow ripe, but domesticated peas remain inside their pods and "wait for the harvester." Corn needs to be husked. Domesticated grains need to be threshed from the stalk. If humanity stopped threshing and planting wheat for a few years, there would be no wheat left. Only the ancient wild cousins of wheat, dropping their seeds as they ripen, would survive.

People who gathered wild plants must have preferred those that ripened slowly, because plants that had not yet spilled out their seeds and grains provided more food for the gatherers. As the gatherers began to save and plant some of these late-ripening grains, the seeds would produce more late-ripening plants. Over many generations, gardeners bred the early-ripening tendency out of the plants they grew. The plants became dependent on human assistance, just as the humans grew dependent on the plants. By storing and replanting seeds they had gathered from wild plants, Middle Eastern people gradually produced the world's first domesticated grain crops: wheat, rye, and barley.

At the same time, these villagers were also beginning to domesticate animals. They probably started with wild animals that they captured and held in pens. The wildest of these, the ones most difficult to keep, would be the first ones slaughtered for meat. The tamer ones would survive longer, and would produce tamer young animals. Gradually, penned wild animals began to allow themselves to be fed, milked, and bred under human supervision. Villagers of the Middle East seem to have domesticated herds of cattle, goats, sheep, and donkeys about the same time they domesticated the first crops. They were becoming the first farmers in the history of the world.

Agriculture seems to have been invented in towns, and later moved to the countryside once the techniques had been perfected. But towns could serve other purposes too. Some became trading centers for tools and treasures: spear points, shells, jewels, and precious metals.

The hunters and gatherers had been skillful makers of clothes and fishing nets and carrying bags. Villagers continued these ancient traditions, but they added new skills. They began to weave cloth from the fibers of the cotton plant, perhaps first in India. Later, as sheep and goats were domesticated, they learned to spin animal hair into yarn. In many places around the world, villagers began to experiment with pottery. The hunter-gatherers had made clay figures, sometimes with brilliant artistry, for many thousands of years. After the pottery wheel was invented in the Middle East, about eight thousand years ago, villagers could shape bowls and vessels to store their food crops. Soon they were making clay bricks and other building materials. Pottery developed independently around the world, wherever hunting peoples had a chance to settle down and experiment with new crafts and skills.

Was this a story of constant progress? No. Most hunter-gatherers did not long to be farmers, and they were often healthier and more free than people tied to the endless labor of tending crops and animals. But where the climate and soil were good, an area that supported ten hunter-gatherers could support a thousand farmers. Once hunter-gatherers began farming, their populations grew rapidly. Families soon depended on their crops and herds. They could not give up farming and go back to hunting and gathering, because there were too many of them — more than the land would support.

The Rice Growers of China

The Yellow River and the Chang (Yangtze) River, the two great rivers of China, are among the longest rivers in the world. Each rises in the mountains in far western China and flows in a mostly easterly direction for some three thousand miles (4,800 kilometers) to the Pacific Ocean. Each river feeds and fertilizes a vast plain. These river valleys became the homes of the ancestral Chinese. At first, the people there were hunters and gatherers who lived amid mammoths and tapirs and giant sloths. Later, after the climate warmed and those Ice Age creatures died off, they hunted wild goats and pigs and other animals more familiar to us. They benefited from the rich bounty of plants native to the river valleys. At least fourteen thousand years ago, hunters and gatherers were collecting food plants throughout the Chang basin.

About 6000 BCE, soon after the villagers of the Middle East began developing wheat and other crops from local wild grains, the people living along the Chang began a similar process with a water-loving wild grass called *oryza*. The evolution of *oryza* into rice was at least as slow and complex as the evolution of wheat, but eventually rice became totally dependent on human cultivation. In the Yellow River valley, where the climate was cooler and rainfall was less abundant, the favored crop was a grain called "millet." (Millet is not as well-known as rice, but it grows well in dry conditions and is still eaten in China, India, and Africa.)

As the Chinese population grew, there were soon more people than hunting and gathering would support. Now their lives depended on the success of the millet crop, or on the delicate, labor-intensive

BIRD'S NEST SOUP

The Chinese filled out their diet with unusual ingredients like birds' nests. Certain species of birds called "swifts" build nests from strings of their own sticky saliva (spit), which hardens as it dries. The nests are collected and used to make soups and desserts. The bird spit gives the dishes a jelly-like texture that is highly prized. It's not clear whether bird's nest soup is good for the health, as many people claim, but it's not all that good for the swifts; in some areas their population has fallen because people keep taking their nests.

work in the rice paddies (fields), which had to be flooded, planted, fertilized, tended, drained, and harvested in just the right sequence. In some parts of the world where farming developed early, the land has now been overcultivated and has turned to desert. But the Chinese have successfully kept growing rice on the same lands for eight thousand years. As the population of China continued to grow, people moved out of the wetlands where *oryza* first grew and began growing rice on terraced hills – turning steep hillsides into "staircases" of tiny parallel fields. In parts of China, thousands of years of rice cultivation have reshaped the whole landscape into rice terraces. Today rice is the most important food crop in the world. The humble millet and rice plants became the foundation of the great civilization of China.

The Three Sisters of the Americas

Plant corn, beans, and squash separately, and they will likely grow well enough. Plant all three together, and each plant will grow even better. Squashes and beans produce nutrients that feed corn plants, and the stalks of the corn are like natural trellises for the beans to climb. Thousands of years ago, farmers in Mexico, in Peru, and later in other regions of the Americas began to plant and harvest these "three sisters." The Aztecs and Mayas of Mexico, the Incas of Peru, the Mound Builders of the Mississippi Valley, and the longhouse people of the Great Lakes region of North America — these great civilizations were built on the simple but fundamental discovery of the "three sisters."

The ancestor of corn or maize is a wild grass called "teosinte" that looks nothing like corn. It does not have strong stalks supporting heavy cobs laden with yellow kernels. But although it provided no more food than stalks of wild grass, Mexican villagers began to plant and tend and harvest teosinte. Over many centuries, they selected those teosinte plants that had larger seeds and heavier stalks, and what had once looked like flurries of seeds on stems of grass slowly grew into small cobs, perhaps as large as your thumb. Over many generations of careful breeding, those cobs grew larger and the stalks became taller and stronger. At the same time, the pioneering farmers of the Americas domesticated wild beans and wild squashes, and discovered that they thrived best when planted together.

As in the Middle East and China, some hunter-gatherers of the Americas began to settle, to tend crops, and to trade. As their villages developed and their populations grew, they too found they could no longer live without the crops that now sustained them. Around the Americas, other plants were tended and slowly domesticated: potatoes and yams in Peru, tobacco farther north. People in the Andes of South America also domesticated animals, particularly the llama, which became a beast of burden as well as a source of wool, milk, and meat.

Herders of the Plains and Steppes

Once there were rivers and pools surrounded by lush green forests in the midst of what is now Africa's Sahara desert. Farther south, the land was fertile but dry, and people who lived there began to tend animals. Around 7500 BCE, some Africans were penning sheep in caves and slowly domesticating them. Others captured and gradually domesticated cattle, and still others trained camels to serve them. These were animals who traveled in herds in the wild, following a leader, and it was fairly natural for them to accept a human in place of an animal as their leader. Eventually these herd animals became a precious source of meat, milk, hides, and wool for herding people. Africans may have been the world's first herders – people who were still nomadic, still migrating and living lightly upon the land, without any permanent villages or towns.

Moving across the dry grasslands with their cattle and goats, herding peoples were not quite farmers, but they had a more secure supply of food than hunters had. Herding became an important way of life in many parts of the world. But not all herding peoples settled for the quiet, simple life of shepherds with their flocks. Some became conquerors.

North of the Black Sea, 2,500 years ago, the Scythians ruled the shortgrass prairie that stretches eastward from Ukraine into Central Asia.

They were people of the horse. It was probably in their part of the world that humans first tamed horses from wild herds and learned to ride them. The Scythians' horses gave them meat and milk, but also carried them far and wide. Scythian men, women, and even children rode constantly. The strength and speed of their horseback armies made them fierce and successful conquerors. Scythian kings grew rich, particularly from the capture and sale of slaves, and the ancient Greeks marveled at the golden jewelry the wild Scythians wore. But even the richest Scythians built only temporary residences. Their home was on the open steppes (plains). Their only monuments were the tombs where they were buried, richly ornamented with gold.

A thousand years later, the Scythians' successors as the great horseback peoples of the Eurasian plains were the Mongols. Like the Scythians long before them, they were fierce warriors and they ranged far and wide. In 1206 CE, Genghis Khan, born in a skin tent on the plains of Mongolia, united the Mongols and sent their mounted armies east, west, and south. The Mongol hordes swept across much of central Asia. They conquered and destroyed Baghdad and Damascus, two capitals of farming civilizations of the Middle East, and they swept into Europe and Russia. Genghis Khan's grandson Kublai Khan was even more successful. Kublai fought with his brother over who would be khan (ruler) of all the Mongols, and the short-lived Mongol empire began to fall to pieces. But Kublai conquered China, and in 1271, he declared himself emperor of China and founder of a new imperial dynasty called the Yuan.

THE BEGINNING OF PAPERWORK

Complex societies need to keep records, and it's hard to do that without paper. The Egyptians learned to write on papyrus, flat sheets made from the pressed stems of reeds. But it was the Chinese who learned to make real paper, by pounding plants and other materials to a pulp, around two thousand years ago. Back then, everything had to be written by hand; if two copies were needed, the whole text had to be written out twice. Some people spent their whole working lives copying other people's writings, page after page, book after book.

Herding peoples have thrived in many parts of the world. When horses first came to the American continents with European invaders around 1500 CE, plains peoples like the Cheyenne, the Sioux, and the Plains Cree quickly became horseback nations, and for a couple of hundred years they ranged the vast prairies of western North America, hunting the bison herds. Just a few hundred years ago, the Sami people of northern Norway and Sweden became the first people in history to tame and domesticate the reindeer that our ancestors hunted for tens of thousands of years, and today there are still Sami who live with reindeer herds that provide them with meat and milk. In Europe today, there are sheep and goat herders who tend their flocks far up in the mountains and come down only to trade with the farmers below, and in the Himalaya mountains of Asia, yak herders scrape a living from the high mountain pastures.

Hunters and Farmers

At the start of the twenty-first century, the few remaining hunter-gatherers of the world live in what most of us consider the world's harshest landscapes: Inuit (Eskimo) in the icy realms of far northern North America, San bushmen in Africa's dry Kalahari desert, aboriginal Australians in the bone-dry outback, and little-known tribes deep in the rainforest jungles of central Africa and Brazil. Yet, while the farming peoples who have taken over the rest of the world may see such places as almost uninhabitable, few of these hunter-gatherers regret their lives, or dream of becoming farmers.

Hunting and gathering is a good life. Those who practice it acquire more food with less effort than almost any other people in the world. Most hunting peoples have been taller, stronger, healthier, and longer-lived than those who fed themselves by farming. Hunters lived well by having few wants, rather than by having many possessions.

Societies that made the transition from hunting to farming paid a price. Farmers had to work harder. They became tied to a single place. Crowded together, they were more likely to suffer from epidemics, including very dangerous diseases that they caught from the animals they lived with so closely. Because they accumulated more possessions than hunters did, farmers knew greater inequalities between rich and poor. Because they owned farms and herds and buildings and other property, they had more to worry about.

But it was farming, which supported far more people than hunting and gathering, that allowed the human species to begin an explosive growth in population. It was farming that allowed humans to own and dominate the world that the hunters and gatherers first walked out into.

With the rise of farming, dense populations could live permanently wherever fertile soil, sufficient rainfall, and agricultural knowledge came together. In Africa and the Americas, in Asia and in Europe, farming people embarked on most of the things we consider "history": cities, kingdoms, and nations, wars and empires, and organized religions; a thousand different cultures, a thousand great traditions in art and literature and philosophy. Dense populations – farming populations – made civilization possible.

All of us have farmers in our family trees. Ten thousand years of farming have made the human species what it is today. Still, we ought not to forget those older ancestors of ours, the hunters and gatherers – small groups around a campfire, laughing and eating and telling stories, ready to fold their tents in the morning and walk up the high passes and down into the valleys, following the animals, praying to the animal spirits to be generous, waiting for whatever nature provides.

CHAPTER THREE

The GOLDEN EMPIRES
5000 BCE — 1000 CE

His birth name was Ying Zheng, but he was known by the name of his kingdom. He was called "Qin," pronounced "Chin" (it's the root of our word "China"). When he inherited the throne of Qin in 247 BCE, he was just thirteen years old, and his kingdom was one of seven that had been fighting for years for control of China. For more than a thousand years, kingdoms and dynasties had risen and fallen in China. Qin's goal was to conquer the rival kingdoms and place all of China under his rule.

The Mayan people of Mexico and Central America played a complicated and sometimes deadly game with a rubber ball. The game was part of their religion, and every Mayan city had ball courts.

Year after year, armies clashed in the fertile river valleys of China. Sometimes as many as one million soldiers were in the field, marching, fighting, and devastating the countryside. In 221 BCE, in the midst of terrible slaughter, the last of Qin's enemies yielded to him. Qin became the first emperor of the whole of China, an emperor with more subjects than any before him. There would be many more wars and dynastic upheavals and invasions, but in Qin's time China was one empire under one ruler. For most of the next two thousand years, uniting China under a single leader would be the ambition of every dynasty.

TRUNG NHI AND TRUNG TRAC

Vietnam was one of the regions cruelly oppressed by the Chinese. When the Trung sisters (about 12 CE–43 CE) were girls, they longed for their country to be free, and they studied war and martial arts. Trung Trac married a young warrior who hoped to overthrow the Chinese overlords. When the Chinese executed him, the sisters led a successful rebellion, with an army mostly of women, and became Vietnam's sister-queens. Their triumph was short-lived – after three years China seized control again, and held Vietnam for centuries. The sisters committed suicide rather than be captured. Vietnam still honors them, with temples and a national holiday in their name.

Qin renamed himself Shi Huangdi, First Emperor, lord of "all under heaven." To keep fifty million people together under his rule, he relied on power, not kindness or love. He did not share his power with any barons and dukes. There would be no hereditary leaders other than him. He divided China into thirty-six districts, each run by a governor and other officials whom he appointed. His word was law, and to make sure no one read about different ideas, he had most of the books in his kingdom burned. Shi Huangdi even outlawed the teachings of the wise philosopher Confucius, who had taught that a king should rule by wisdom and example, not by force.

In war, Shi Huangdi commanded hundreds of thousands of soldiers. It was the same in peacetime. Every household in the empire was obliged to provide sons as soldiers, and taxes for the emperor's use. With these resources, the emperor ordered national roads built to unify his domains. He had canals and dams constructed along the Yellow River and the Chang. To secure his northern boundaries against "barbarians" — meaning anyone beyond his empire — he ordered the building of a wall, one of the first parts of the Great Wall of China. He established a new legal code for his empire. He created the first money for all of China. He directed that all his subjects must use the same script to write the various languages of China. Over the next two thousand years, China would keep many of the features introduced by Shi Huangdi to hold his kingdom together.

THE GREAT WALL OF CHINA

Ancient towns and cities were often surrounded by high walls to keep enemies out. Sometime in the 200s BCE, the emperor of China resolved to do even better: he would build a wall of earth and stone across his land. The wall was several stories high, and wide enough that horses could gallop along the top. It had guard-houses where soldiers lived, and towers where they watched for invaders. Later emperors improved the wall until it stretched more than fifteen hundred miles (2,400 kilometers). Even so, the claim that you can see it from space is an exaggeration.

This emperor who controlled the lives of millions of people lived in splendor at his capital city of Xianyang, while most Chinese were poor peasant farmers living close to their rice paddies. Shi Huangdi died in 210 BCE, at the age of fifty, but he intended to rule even from the grave.

He had laid his plans well. Hundreds of thousands of his people had labored for decades to build his tomb near Xianyang. When he died, Shi Huangdi was buried with his treasures, not in a grave, but in a kind of eternal palace. Everything he needed to rule the afterlife forever was buried alongside him. To serve and protect him there, he had an army buried with him: the Terracotta Army.

The Terracotta Army was eight thousand soldiers sculpted from clay ("terracotta" means "cooked earth"). Each soldier was unique and larger than life, with his own realistic face and posture. Each was equipped with armor and weapons, and some rode in terracotta chariots drawn by terracotta horses. The soldiers stand in formation across several miles around Shi Huangdi's palace, proclaiming the eternal authority of the man who had ruled the world's greatest empire.

But Shi Huangdi's dynasty lasted only a few years. Soon after his death, his empire collapsed in civil war. The Qin dynasty was replaced by another. New kings moved away from Xianyang, and Shi Huangdi's palace was burned to the ground. The Terracotta Army was buried in the ruins, each figure still bearing its soldierly expression of loyalty and courage. Standing silently on guard in their underground tomb, the soldiers were lost and forgotten for two thousand years. Then, in 1974, some farmers drilling a well discovered them. Today the Terracotta Army and the First Emperor's tomb have become one of China's — and the world's — most magnificent heritage sites. Archeologists continue to excavate and study the tomb. People come from across the world to the modern city of Xi'an to admire the power, artistry, and ambition of what was one of the world's great empires.

THE CELESTIAL TORTOISE

According to Chinese tradition, four animals — dragon, phoenix, unicorn, and tortoise (land turtle) — are important symbols of good luck, and together they govern the four cardinal points of the compass. The tortoise — the only one of the four that actually exists — is the ruler of the north, and a symbol of strength, endurance, and longevity. (Not surprising — have you ever seen a young-looking turtle?) Although tortoises are real animals, the symbolic tortoise is often shown with fantastic features like dragon ears, flaming tentacles, and a long, hairy tail.

39

Sumeria

The world's first empires arose where people had settled down and learned to be farmers. These are the places where we find the earliest civilizations and the first shahs, emperors, pharaohs, and other rulers of empires. When people tended herds and grew crops, they soon found that their fields, livestock, stored food, and even the homes they built were tempting targets for thieves, for raiders, for conquering armies. Societies became more organized, and the first governments arose. Some societies were city-states — usually a single city and the farming region around it. Others were nations where a single ruler commanded a territory stretching over vast areas, and where most people lived in the countryside, not in cities.

Possibly the very first human civilization developed in a region called Mesopotamia (now in Iraq), between the Tigris and Euphrates rivers at one end of the "fertile crescent" that curves from Egypt's Nile River, across the Middle East, to the Persian Gulf. One early city there was called Sumer, and the people became known as Sumerian. Their civilization arose more than seven thousand years ago, yet many of its features would have seemed familiar to most people until just a few hundred years ago, when the industrial age began.

Most people in Sumeria grew crops and raised animals and lived the hard, plain lives of farmers. But as agriculture thrived, the city could also support people who were not farmers. There were potters, who made the jars and vessels in which crops were stored, and tanners, who prepared animal hides for clothing, and weavers, who worked with linen and other fabrics. Brewers and bakers supplied the city's tables. Metalworkers produced bronze and iron that let Sumerians perform tasks more effectively than people who still depended on stone tools. Jewelers worked gold and silver and produced elaborate beadwork from

REEDS AND CLAY

Around 3300 BCE, the Sumerians began pressing a reed with a triangular end (called a *cuneus*) against a block of soft clay to make lines and triangles that meant numbers and letters, in a system called "cuneiform." Then they baked the clay till it hardened into a permanent record that could be sent from person to person. Cuneiform probably started as a form of bookkeeping – "6 sheep 2 goats." It soon developed into a more general writing system, but only a few privileged people were allowed to learn it.

ceramic and shells. Builders assembled not only farmers' huts, but palaces and tall temples called "ziggurats" that made Sumer one of the early wonders of the world. Engineers designed canals, dams, locks, and sluices that irrigated the farmlands. Merchants and traders brought precious goods like deep blue indigo dye from India. Sailors plied the rivers and the shores of the Persian Gulf. It may have been some Sumerian genius who figured out how to use wheels, for Sumer was among the first places on earth with chariots and wagons to carry people and goods.

The people of Sumer, at least some of them, could read and write. Indeed, they and their neighbors seem to have invented one of the world's first writing systems. They probably began by marking clay tablets to keep track of animals, crops, and other supplies in the royal storehouses of the city, but slowly a written script was developed. Once they were able to store and transmit information this way, they moved on to mathematics and geometry. They made a science of astronomy and developed a calendar based on careful observations of the sun and moon. Sumer and its rival city-states supported music, art, and literature, and some of the stories they told, like the *Epic of Gilgamesh*, are among the oldest we have. Even a statue of the hero Gilgamesh survives, holding one of the lions he defeated.

Not all the discoveries the Sumerians made were happy ones. Farming societies soon had rich and poor, nobles and commoners. The powerful declared that it was their right to own and protect the vital farmland; other people would have to support them with their labor and their crops. As in Shi Huangdi's China centuries later, royal power made it possible to build great monuments: canals, temples, and palaces that required the well-organized labor of tens of thousands of people over many years. But it meant inequality and oppression too. Most people in Sumer, as in China and Egypt and other early civilizations, were farmers ruled by a handful of nobles and priests and generals. Early civilizations often allowed slavery, and sometimes even the poor farmers were little better than slaves. While Sumer's godlike kings became enormously wealthy and lived in great splendor, most farming families eked out a living in small mud huts near the fields and pastures.

Civilization also brought wars. Hunting peoples fought each other, true — but rich farmlands, grand cities, and prosperous trade routes offered far more temptation for war. In much the same way that they organized workers to build cities and monuments, kings organized soldiers to fight for their cities and empires. Highly trained Sumerian troops marched and fought across the Mesopotamian plains. The infantry wielded carefully made bronze spears, and the cavalry swept forward in war chariots, under the command of generals whose written orders could convey their will over long distances. Many cities that first emerged to show humanity's brilliance in planning and building ended their days in fire and plunder and destruction, as conquering armies slaughtered the men and carried off the women and children as slaves.

With civilization, too, came epidemic diseases, often beginning with farm animals, but spreading rapidly through crowded settlements. Polio, measles, smallpox, plague — all the terrible diseases against which people remained nearly helpless for thousands of years — were part of the inheritance of civilization.

Not long after Sumerian civilization began, Indian societies with mysterious names like Mohenjo-Daro ("the mound of the dead") and Harappa arose in the valley of the Indus River. Around the same time, Egyptian civilization began to emerge along Africa's mighty Nile River.

Ancient Egypt

Across the Nile River, following the sun from east to west, came the Pharaoh Hatshepsut in her golden boat. Each spring, the Nile flooded its banks to pour fresh nutrients across the low-lying farmlands all along its shores. Year after year, the Nile fed the people who lived along it, and the Egyptian population grew, until an immensely rich civilization filled the valley. Hatshepsut, absolute ruler of this river empire, was crossing the Nile to the Valley of the Kings. There, she would thank the gods who had brought prosperity to her people. There, too, she would inspect the vast and beautiful temple she was having built in the Valley of the Kings, one of the most spectacular burying places anywhere in the world.

THE GREAT PYRAMID OF GIZA

Egypt has many pyramids, but the biggest is the Great Pyramid of Giza. Hidden deep inside it is the burial chamber of the pharaoh Khufu (also called Cheops), who ruled Egypt around 2680 BCE. Built of immense limestone blocks, and polished to a shine on the outside, the pyramid gleamed bright white under the blazing sun. At 482 feet (147 meters), it remained the world's tallest building for four thousand years. Khufu himself disappeared long ago, when his burial chamber was raided by grave-robbers.

43

Hatshepsut had been born into the eighteenth dynasty of Egyptian rulers. In her day, in the mid-1400s BCE, Egyptian civilization was already ancient. The great pyramids of Giza, the burial monuments of much earlier pharaohs, were already more than a thousand years old. Like Hatshepsut, those rulers had been gods to their people. But the first pharaohs must

THE BEASTS OF BAST

The Egyptians associated many animals with gods, but cats were especially revered because they protected precious grain and other foods from rats and snakes. They were sacred to the kindly cat-goddess Bast, who was the daughter of the sun-god Ra, and the symbol of the sun's life-giving warmth. (Think of how cats like to curl up in a warm patch of sunlight!) But being sacred wasn't always a good thing. Cats were sacrificed as offerings to the gods, and their little bodies were turned into mummies, and given elaborate burials. In 1888 an Egyptian farmer discovered a large tomb near the Nile, containing the mummies of almost 80,000 cats.

have begun as military leaders, controlling the farmlands, taxing the harvest, maintaining order, and defending their territory against enemies. Pharaohs ruled by their power and authority, and though they traced their ancestry through the female side of the family, they passed their kingship down to men, usually to their sons. If a pharaoh did not grow his own beard, he wore a fake ceremonial one on his chin. It was one of the symbols of his authority as a man.

Yet Hatshepsut, a woman of grace and beauty, became a pharaoh. She was the only surviving child of Thutmose, a mighty ruler. Hatshepsut's husband got his power from being married to Thutmose's daughter, and she ruled alongside him. When he died, Hashepsut took power in the name of her stepson, but she soon proclaimed herself Pharaoh, declaring that her true father was the god Amun, creator and sustainer of the world. Hatshepsut ruled for twenty years. She even wore the ceremonial beard to make clear that she might be a woman but she was also the Pharaoh of Egypt.

Hatshepsut's reign was a time of glory for Egypt. A "New Kingdom" had emerged from an era of wars, foreign invasions, and weak monarchs. Her father's military campaigns had restored Egypt's power and enriched the country. Taxes were flowing into the royal treasuries. Hatshepsut sent army expeditions to maintain Egypt's borders and repel its enemies. She sent ships to build trade with a southern land known as Punt. And she commissioned some of Egypt's greatest buildings. Throughout the history of the Egyptian empire, most people lived in the country-side, growing crops along the banks of the Nile. Only the pharaoh, his family, his servants, his priests, and his administrators lived in the royal capital. During the New Kingdom, this capital city was Thebes, on the east bank of the Nile, with its lavish palaces and vast temples of Karnak and Luxor. Across the river, where the sun set, lay the Valley of the Kings. Hatshepsut's husband and her father had their tombs there. Hatshepsut ordered her architects to build her a mortuary temple at the gateway to the Valley. It would be one of the most beautiful and symmetrical creations of ancient history. Many of the greatest pharaohs of Egypt would build their own monuments in the valley Hatshepsut had developed.

After Hatshepsut died, her stepson Thutmose III finally took power in his own name. He grew into a strong and successful monarch, and he decided to erase the record of the stepmother who had kept him from the throne, striking her name from monuments and statues wherever he could. Nevertheless, he and many of his successors, including the mighty conqueror Ramses the Great and the boy pharaoh Tutankhamen, chose the Valley of the Kings as their burial place. They had their tombs constructed beyond Hatshepsut's spectacular temple at the entrance to the valley. Despite Thutmose III, the name and fame of Hatshepsut the female pharaoh would not be lost.

The World of the Mayas

Far across the oceans from the city-states and empires of China, the Middle East, and Egypt, the Americas developed their own glittering civilizations. Seventeen hundred years ago, they were playing ball in the sacred ball court at Tikal, and they were playing for their lives.

Tikal was one of many city-states of the Mayan people, whose civilization spread across the highlands and lowlands of Central America and southern Mexico from 1000 BCE to 1000 CE. In its day, Tikal was a city of at least sixty thousand people, and one of the largest and most powerful Mayan city-states. Over the centuries, Tikal's people had transformed the deep green rainforests of the lowlands around their city into pale green fields of corn. All the Mayan city-states were like this: cities of poor farming people who spent their lives tending the corn in the surrounding fields.

But while most of Tikal's people were poor, Tikal itself was wealthy. As long as their food supplies were secure, Mayan city-states grew rich and proud and powerful. Traders from Tikal ranged all across Central America, exchanging goods with other cities and bringing back treasures to the city's rulers: pearls, jade, obsidian, and gold. Tikal's armies marched down fine white Mayan roads to keep the city's subject peoples in obedience, or to gather tribute and slaves by waging war.

Tikal had no river or lake nearby. It would only prosper as long as the rains came, for the crops that fed its people and provided the city's wealth needed water constantly. To secure the water supply, even in seasons of drought, Tikal relied on a network of reservoirs and canals and dams laboriously constructed all around the city. It took careful organization to build and maintain the canal system, so the elite of nobles and priests who ran the city-state could demand absolute loyalty from the farmers who depended on the water.

But Tikal had more than canals and dams. It was a beautiful city of broad plazas and avenues lined with lavish palaces and soaring pyramid-temples. The city and its pyramids were carefully aligned to the stars, for the Mayas were masters of mathematics and astronomy. Their engineers and architects built structures as spectacular as any in the ancient world. Their scribes developed writing and one of the world's most elaborate and complex calendars, which could precisely calculate the past and future of the Mayan world over millions of years.

Rich farmland, splendid engineering, and brilliant science did not guarantee peace to the people of Tikal. The Mayan city-states were frequently at war with each other. Life was often brutal, violent, and short. The records of Tikal show that in 378 CE, the armies of Jaguar Paw, lord of Tikal, were defeated by the general Fire Is Born, leader of an invading army from Teotihuacán, a great city of another civilization in the faraway Valley of Mexico. Jaguar Paw died the day the enemy conquered his city. Was he killed in battle, or sacrificed to his enemies' gods? Or did he kill himself in shame and despair? Whatever happened, Tikal and many other Mayan cities were ruled by Teotihuacán for years after that. During that time, many northern, Mexican traditions were incorporated into Mayan art and science.

Tikal and the other Mayan cities eventually threw off the yoke of conquest, and the glories of their civilization continued for many more centuries. As Tikal grew and prospered, the people devoted more and more energy to a kind of substitute for war: the ball game.

Rubber grows naturally in the forests around there, and people learned to play with bouncing rubber balls — something that would amaze later visitors from Europe. The Mayan ball game was played with a heavy rubber ball in a long narrow court with hoops high on the side walls. Players hit the ball with their shoulders, hips, and forearms, playing by rules we hardly understand. But this became more than a game. Every Mayan city had ball courts near the ceremonial heart of the city — Tikal had seven of them. The game became part of the Mayan religion, in which people prayed to the gods of the cornfields, the gods of water, and the gods of war. It also became part of the rivalry between the city-states, for they sometimes competed on the ball court rather than on the battlefield.

CHICHÉN ITZÁ

Sometime around 500 CE — long before Europeans arrived in the Americas — the Mayas built the city of Chichén Itzá in southeastern Mexico, as a major religious and political center. In the middle of the city is a pyramid dedicated to Quetzalcoatl, a feathered snake-god. On the spring and fall equinoxes — the two days of the year when night and day are the same length — sunlight and shadows on one side of the pyramid suggest a snake slithering down to meet a huge stone snake-head carved at the bottom.

Mayan religion was as fierce as Mayan warfare. The city needed rain and the kings needed conquests, and as the price of their divine support, the gods needed human blood. Some of it was supplied by kings and priests who pierced themselves and offered up their own blood. More came from human sacrifices. High atop the gleaming pyramids, the hearts of war captives and other victims were cut out and offered to the gods. Somehow, the ball games became part of these bloody rituals, and the losing players sometimes paid with their lives.

The Mayas were not the only early civilization in the Americas. In time, knowledge of corn-growing spread north and south. Farming societies arose in the fertile Mississippi valley of North America. Down in South America, in the highlands of Ecuador and Peru, the Inca civilization was the greatest of many that rose and flourished and fell over the centuries.

The Mwene Mutapa

Many of Africa's oldest and largest societies arose south of the Sahara desert in West Africa, among herders and farmers. But one African civilization left a monument in southeastern Africa, where for seven hundred years the ruined city called Great Zimbabwe has brooded over the rolling grasslands of the high plateau between the Limpopo and Zambezi rivers. Who built its stone towers and mighty walls?

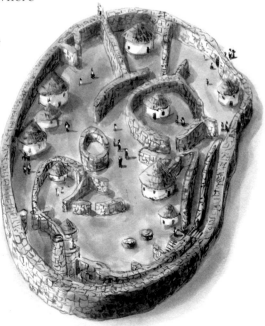

The Mwene Mutapa built them, or had them built. Mwene Mutapa means "lords of the conquered lands." Around 1300 CE, the Mwene Mutapa came from the north with their armies and their cattle and their iron-tipped spears, and the seeds of their crops of sorghum, millet, and yams. They took control of this rich and fertile land, and of the gold in the rivers that cut through the high plateau.

49

Gold – so easy to work, so bright and beautiful when refined and polished – has been loved by nearly all those who have discovered it. The people called Mwene Mutapa soon found trading partners eager to buy the gold they gathered. They developed a thriving trade down to a seaport named Sofala, near the mouth of the Zambezi River on the Indian Ocean. Arab sailors and traders came down the coast to Sofala every year to trade for Zimbabwean gold. In exchange, they brought fabrics across the ocean from India, even ceramics from distant China. These goods traveled up into the interior of Africa to adorn the lords and ladies of the Mwene Mutapa. At the heart of their new empire, the kings of the Mwene Mutapa built their city. Great Zimbabwe's stone walls and high towers inspired awe and respect among the herders and hunters of the plateau. For many years, those walls and towers protected the Mwene Mutapa against all rivals.

Then the gold began to run out. The Mwene Mutapa had gathered all the gold they could easily find in the rivers, but they had never discovered the deep mineral seams from which the gold eroded into the rivers. Without the gold trade, they could no longer support traders, artisans, armies, and kings. Gradually, Great Zimbabwe was abandoned, around the time that European explorers came into the Indian Ocean and disrupted the ancient networks of trade routes there. After a few hundred years of wealth and power, the Mwene Mutapa people moved on, leaving the ruins of their city to amaze and puzzle later travelers.

Great Zimbabwe's decline was not unique. Many early societies, even empires, have failed and collapsed, all over the world. The very earliest civilizations, in Mesopotamia, gradually destroyed the soil that they cultivated. The ground grew barren and turned to desert, dooming the glittering cities and the great kings of Sumer and the other city-states of Mesopotamia. Tikal and the other Mayan cities fell from splendor into ruin in just a few centuries, between about 700 and 900 CE. A period of drought is probably what killed them. The jungle soils were thin and water was scarce, for the rains only nourished the Mayan lands for a few months each year. When there was not enough rain to fill the canals and reservoirs that watered the crops, the city died. People starved or moved on, and the rainforest grew over the farms, the great plaza, the ball courts, even the pyramids. For many years, Tikal was a lost city. Many great rulers have built cities and empires they thought would last forever. Most of those cities and empires have vanished from the earth, leaving only stories, mysterious ruins, and legends of lost treasure.

ANGKOR WAT

Another spectacular city that was lost for centuries is Angkor Wat. In the early 1100s CE, the lord of Cambodia's Khmer Empire decided to build an immense temple-city, surrounded by a moat, dedicated to the Hindu god Vishnu. But not long after it was built, the city was sacked by the Cham people of Vietnam. The ruins became overgrown by jungle and were almost forgotten until the late 1800s, when archeologists discovered them. The sculptures of Angkor Wat, with its gates and towers and statues, give us a wonderful look into the life of the Khmer people so long ago.

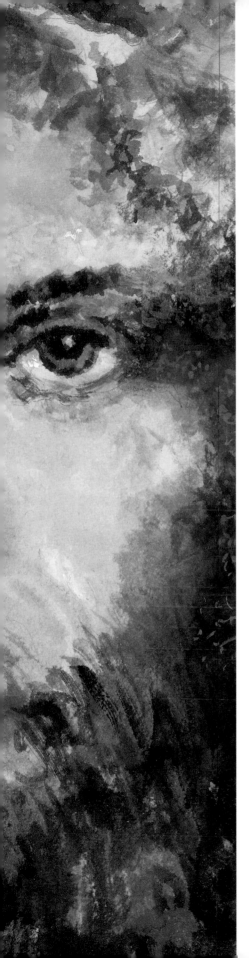

CHAPTER FOUR

GODS *and* LAWGIVERS
5000 BCE — 1000 CE

When people live together, they need rules. But who makes the rules?

"An eye for an eye; a tooth for a tooth." About 1750 BCE – thousands of years after the rise and fall of the city-state of Sumer, and a few hundred years before Hatshepsut ruled as pharaoh in Egypt – Hammurabi was king of Babylon, and Babylon was the most powerful empire in Mesopotamia. Few people today would remember him for that; the empire of Babylon soon vanished, like many others before and after it. But Hammurabi's name and portrait can be found in courthouses all over the world. The reason? In the plaza in Babylon, Hammurabi had a tall stone monument inscribed with 282 laws that everyone in his kingdom had to obey.

Where did early people get rules to live by? From religious figures like the Hindu elephant-god Ganesh (left) or the Christian Jesus (right), or from leaders like Hammurabi (center).

Hammurabi's code was written in the language of the people, and available to all who could read. (Not so many could.) It declared that accused persons should be considered innocent until their crimes were proven, and set out a list of rules and punishments based on the principle that the punishment should fit the crime. This code, now almost four thousand years old, was one of the first to decree the rules by which a nation should govern itself. Hammurabi was an absolute ruler who believed he had been chosen by the Babylonian gods. He was a warrior king who conquered many of the city-states around Babylon. But his idea that people should live according to a clear and unchanging set of laws was a great and powerful one. Every civilization that tries to live by a code of written laws, applied to all its citizens, is continuing the dream of Hammurabi.

Long before people had law codes, they had gods. For tens of thousands of years, human beings respected and feared the power of nature, and tried to win nature's goodwill. They honored the power of nature in thunder, on the heights of mountains, in deep caves, in the spirits of mighty animals. Hunting peoples sought a bond with the animals they hunted, so that their trackers would find the trail and their arrows would fly true. As people took up farming, they trusted their lives to the givers of crops. Sometimes these were earth goddesses, the mothers of corn or rice, who looked lovingly on their human children and provided new crops and new life each year, so long as people honored them and gave them thanks. Among both hunters and farmers, a chief was often a priest as well, someone who spoke to the gods on the people's behalf and ruled the people in the name of the gods. In time, kings and emperors were not only priests to the gods, but gods themselves.

As human societies spread around the world, their beliefs developed according to their local conditions and ways of life. Eventually there must have been millions of tribal gods, customs, and faiths that let hunters and farmers seek favor from supernatural powers (often at a great price), and that gave people a code of how they should behave. Most of these tribal faiths remained with the people who began them. A few would blossom into world religions.

Hinduism, the main religion of India, may be the oldest of the great religions of the modern world. Its roots are thousands of years old. Its sacred texts, called the Vedas, may be three thousand years old. Hinduism has many gods and sacred beings, but its constant concern is the human soul. Hindus believe that a soul may be reincarnated (reborn) over and over into new bodies, always seeking to rise higher, away from earthly things, always seeking unity with the cosmic spirit. "Dharma," rightful conduct, helps one's soul to rise, so Hindus practice nonviolence, respect for animals, and often vegetarianism. They respect the wisdom of teachers and sacred texts, but there is no central authority (like a pope) in Hinduism, and there are many varieties of the religion. Today almost a billion people practice Hinduism. Nearly all of them live in India or are of Indian descent. But Hinduism has also brought much to the rest of the world, including yoga and the art of meditation. For Hindus, yoga is a set of methods for seeking wisdom through exercising body and mind. In the Western world, it's often more about exercise than about wisdom. Not all Indians are Hindus; there are also Sikhs, Jains, Parsees, and others.

HOLY COWS

Hindus respect all animals, but especially cattle, a symbol of the earth, abundance, and the sacredness of all life. Lord Krishna, a central figure of Hinduism, is said to have appeared as a cowherd. Traditional Hindus do not eat beef; feeding a cow is an act of worship, and during the harvest festival, people even decorate their cattle with flowers. In New Delhi, India's capital city, cowboys have been hired to gently round up the cattle that wander into the streets and cause monstrous traffic jams.

Another world religion, Buddhism, was also born in India, and it began with a man named Siddhartha Gautama. He was born to a royal family in India about 500 BCE, and he grew up privileged and protected. His father, it is said, sheltered him from all signs of pain and unhappiness. Then one day Siddhartha encountered an old man who was about to die. Siddhartha began to question the meaning of life, and he left home in search of enlightenment. He had lived in luxury and self-indulgence, but neither wealth nor poverty had given him enlightenment. Now he fasted, suffered, and deprived himself of all worldly things. Siddhartha sat down in the shade of a pipil tree and decided not to move until he understood what to do. He sat for forty-five days, and at the end of that time he arose with an understanding of "the middle way," a way of living that would be neither too easy on him nor too harsh, that would bring him enlighten-ment. Siddhartha Gautama became the Buddha, the enlightened one, and he taught by example: what mattered for humanity was to pray, meditate, and come to understand the meaning of life.

The Buddha was not a god, and Buddhists do not worship him. They seek to be like him, to share in his wisdom through prayer and study, and to unite with others on the same path toward enlightenment. Hundreds of years after the Buddha, the Buddhist faith spread out of India into the places it still thrives, particularly in China and Southeast Asia. Shinto, the main religion of Japan, shares common roots with Buddhism. The Dalai Lama is both a teacher of Tibetan Buddhism and a leader of the Tibetan people.

The ancient traditional religion of China is Taoism, but China also saw the rise of Confucianism, based on the teachings of Confucius (really K'ung Fu-tzu, which simply means Master Kung). Confucius, who lived between about 550 BCE and 480 BCE, was not really the prophet of a new religion. He was a philosopher. He thought deeply about how people should behave and how they should treat one another, and about the duties of leaders and followers. Kings, said Confucius, should lead by example, not by fear; they should

cultivate personal virtue as much as power. Elders should give a good example to the young, and the young must respect and learn from their elders. Confucius taught that if people became virtuous and behaved properly, they would not need law codes or punishments to make them treat each other with courtesy and respect.

The ancient Eastern practices of Hinduism, Buddhism, and Confucianism explored self-knowledge and appropriate behavior. Gods were important in these faiths, but the main emphasis was on the human soul and the human mind. The Middle East, however, became the home of three world religions that are all rooted in the idea of a single god, God the Father, who looks down on the world, intervenes in the lives of his people, and judges them. Religions that have just one god are called "monotheistic."

Long before the days of monotheistic religions, people of the eastern Mediterranean had their own national or tribal faiths. The people of ancient Greece worshipped a family of gods rather like the ancient

Greeks themselves: proud, quarrelsome, passionate, and unpredictable. Led by the god Zeus, and living high on Mount Olympus, they interfered as much or as little as they chose in the lives of the people below. The people of Egypt also had many gods, including their ruler, the pharaoh. But the Jews, a minor tribe of migrant shepherds and herders, had only one god. They believed there was a covenant (agreement) between God and the Jews, his "chosen people." If they honored him and followed his will, he would protect and guide them. Although this one god was a supernatural being, he took an interest in his people and expected them to live good lives.

Led by Moses, the Jews eventually settled in the "land of Israel," around the sacred city of Jerusalem, under their own kings and priests. In Jerusalem they built a great temple that became the center of the Jewish religion. But the Jewish homeland fell under the control of the Romans, in the days of the Roman Empire, and about 70 CE the Romans destroyed the temple and scattered the people. Judaism became a religion of exiles. For two thousand years, most Jews lived as a minority among people of other religions. But they always believed that God would intervene and help them, and send the Messiah (Savior). Even today, devout Jews are awaiting the arrival of the Messiah.

Not long after the Jewish state was conquered, a Jewish preacher appeared, by the name of Jesus, and Christianity was born. For Christians, Jesus was the Messiah, the "redeemer," the son of God who had come down to earth to save humanity from its weaknesses. Although Christianity seemed like a branch of Judaism, it reached out to non-Jews with the belief that all people could be "chosen people." At first Christians were persecuted in the Roman Empire, but in time Rome adopted Christianity, and Christianity became the religion of Europe. As Europe became the most powerful part of the world, Christianity grew with it, and Europeans spread Christianity wherever they went.

Until very recently, Christianity was followed by more people than any other religion in the world. But a third religion also bloomed from that Middle Eastern idea of one fatherly god in heaven. Around 600 CE, a prophet and teacher named Muhammad began to preach a new faith to replace the many faiths and gods worshipped by the desert tribes of Arabia. This faith became known as Islam, "submission to Allah," the one god. Followers of Allah, known as Muslims, accept Muhammad as the last prophet of Allah, following the prophets Moses and Jesus. The religion spread with astonishing speed, west across northern Africa, eastward into Mesopotamia, India, and beyond. Islam provided law and government as well as religion. The caliph, the supreme ruler of the Islamic lands in the early centuries of the religion, soon ruled a territory that stretched from Spain and North Africa to the Arabian deserts, across the Middle East, and east to the borders of India. Eventually Islam would gain many believers in China and Southeast Asia as well. Today, Islam has more believers than any other religion.

There are still many other faiths around the world. Sacred images carved on rocks in the Australian desert are tens of thousands of years old, for the faith of the aboriginal peoples there is one of the oldest anywhere. Native American traditions, African religions, and many others remain important to those who have grown up with them. Some people do not accept any religion at all. But six great religions command the allegiance of most of the people in the world: the three one-god faiths that emerged from the Middle East (Judaism, Christianity, and Islam), the two "enlightenment" religions that were born in India (Hinduism and Buddhism), and the Taoist-Confucian religion of China.

Most religions offer a vision of a god or gods who can be contacted by human prayer and sacrifice, and a set of lessons on how people should behave. The dharma codes of Hinduism and Buddhism teach virtuous behavior that assists believers along the path to enlightenment. Confucius's teachings are almost entirely concerned with the best way to live and behave. Moses, the great lawgiver of the Jewish people, brought the Ten Commandments down from a mountaintop in the desert, commanding people to honor God, respect their parents, and reject murder, theft, lying, and other wrongs. The Ten Commandments are part of Judaism, Christianity, and Islam, but for Islam the supreme guide is the Qur'an, which gives Muslims both spiritual teaching and a way of government.

All religions share a sense of a world that exists beyond the everyday material world. Religions appeal to our spiritual feeling, our belief in wonder and in supernatural forces that guide our lives. Yet religions have always been rooted in the earth, just as they were when early farmers worshipped the spirits of corn or rice. Around the world, many sacred places are associated with religious experiences. Some of these are natural places, like Delphi in Greece or Uluru (Ayers Rock) in Australia, places where almost every visitor is struck by a sense of spiritual wonder. Others, like Jerusalem, Mecca, the Vatican City in Italy, or Lhasa in Tibet, are spiritual centers because they have temples, churches, or places of pilgrimage.

Religions help people decide how to behave, and in the past, priest-kings often enforced the religious code and punished those who defied it. When Hammurabi proclaimed his code of laws almost four thousand years ago, he declared that it had been given to him by Shamash, the sun god of the Babylonians. But Hammurabi's code also had courts to enforce it, and rules by which evidence would be presented and judged. The code declared that the king would enforce private contracts that citizens had sworn "before god and the king." Law codes were beginning to reflect not only the commandments of a god, but the rules that would help people get along together, fairly and peacefully, by mutual agreement.

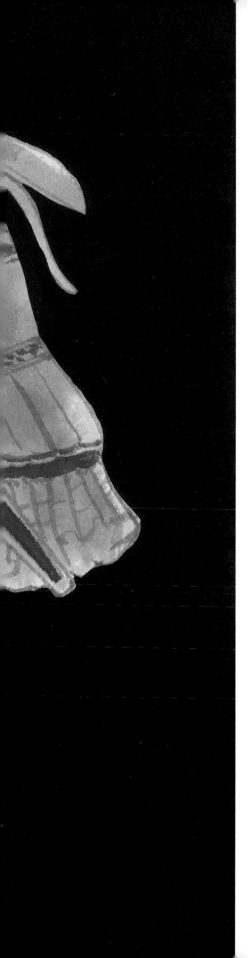

CHAPTER FIVE

The GREEKS and ROMANS
500 BCE — 500 CE

"I am Cyrus, king of the world, great king, legitimate king, king of Babylon, king of Sumer and Akkad, king of the four rims of the world."

In 539 BCE, King Cyrus of Persia had a clay cylinder stamped with these words buried under the temple he was building in Babylon to celebrate his conquest of the city. Cyrus the Persian now ruled Babylon, the great and ancient capital of the Assyrian Empire which had menaced the Persians for centuries. The Persians, once a fighting tribe from the hill country in what is now Iran, had become the new masters of Mesopotamia, that fertile region of the Middle East where civilizations and dynasties had been rising and falling for several thousand years.

Two warriors — Persian (left) and Greek (right) — locked in combat. The shield shows Pegasus, the winged horse of Greek legend.

Cyrus declared himself Shah-an-shah, King of Kings, master of the whole world. His armies conquered Egypt and made the pharaoh kneel before the shah. They conquered ancient cities as far east as India. They marched over high mountains into the endless plains of central Asia, although the horse-backed nomads there mostly melted away as the invaders approached. The Persians surged across Turkey and pushed on to the Black Sea shores of Europe. From every conquest, the armies brought back tribute and treasures to adorn the palaces of the king of the world.

EARLY "AIRMAIL"

As early as biblical times, people put wings on their messages; they sent letters by homing pigeons, which fly home from wherever they are released. The Romans sent military secrets by pigeon; the Greeks sent news of the Olympic Games. Even people who couldn't write could communicate this way. Pigeons flying home from a ship meant that the ship would soon be arriving. A pigeon released by a royal messenger was a warning that the messenger had been attacked. Homing pigeons were still carrying messages until quite recently.

To rule his many distant provinces, the emperor sent out governors called "satraps." These governors made sure that the local people paid taxes to the shah, and they built fortified cities linked by a network of roads to bind his empire together. Cyrus was tolerant of the local peoples' faiths, languages, and customs, so long as they accepted Persian rule. The nations he added to his empire could even keep their own kings, making Cyrus truly a king of kings; he is remembered as Cyrus the Great. Otherwise, he was like the pharaohs, the Chinese emperors, the Mayan lords, and other leaders of empires. They were all "absolute rulers." Their word was law. Those who disobeyed them died. The Persians intended everyone in the world to fear the wrath of the king of kings.

Mighty Persia, Tiny Greece

Only one people in the known world remained beyond the power of the Persian king. These were the Greeks, who lived at the far end of civilization, west of the Persian territory. The Greeks had never had a great empire. Cyrus would barely have thought of them when he proclaimed that his empire stretched to the edge of the world. Still, the Greeks were a proud and stubborn people. Some of them chose to defy the king of all the world.

Greece was not a single state, but a collection of cities and towns. The Greeks took pride in their traditions and arts. Today people still read the ancient Greek story of *The Iliad*, the tale of a terrible war fought by the ancestors of the Greeks against a city called Troy. In *The Iliad*, the gods watch human events, and sometimes take sides, as the Greeks and Trojans fight and love and die: Achilles the peerless warrior, cunning Ulysses, beautiful Helen, and poor Cassandra, who has the gift of seeing the future and the curse of never being believed. *The Iliad* ends when Greek armies conquer and destroy Troy. In another immortal work, *The Odyssey*, Ulysses struggles through ten years of strange adventures as he tries to find his way back to his wife and his home.

By 500 BCE, although Greece meant little to the world compared to the wealth and luxury of Persia, it had become a busy, prosperous collection of city-states, each of them independent and often at war with the others.

THE ROSE-RED CITY OF PETRA

While empires clashed, the business of trade went on. Back in the
300s BCE, some people called Nabateans built the city of Petra inside
a desert canyon, carving some of the buildings right into the canyon's
red sandstone walls. Petra, now in Jordan, was a vital watering stop for
caravans transporting spices and silks and slaves across the desert. It was
well protected from invaders because it was completely hidden, with just
one entrance: a narrow, winding passage through the cliffs. But in
106 CE the Nabateans were defeated by the Romans. Their city was
almost forgotten, until a young Swiss explorer tracked it down in 1812.

Athens, Sparta, Thebes, Corinth, and other cities were on mainland
Greece, but the Greeks, great traders and sailors, had also scattered cities
and colonies across the rocky islands of the Aegean Sea, along the west
coast of Turkey, up into the Black Sea, and as far west as the southern
coasts of Italy.

The Greeks lived in a world dominated by godlike pharaohs,
shahs, and emperors, but in the city of Athens the idea had taken hold that
there should be no king or aristocratic rulers. Instead, all citizens should
share in governing the city. (By "all citizens" the Athenians meant adult
male citizens, not women or foreigners or slaves.) When decisions had to
be made, the citizens gathered in public meetings to debate and vote, and
they abided by the decisions that resulted. They called this system "democracy," from the Greek words *demos*, "people," and *kratos*, "power."

The citizens of Athens decided that they would not submit to the
Persian emperor, who was by this time a king named Darius. When word of
this defiance from some minor, distant village reached the ears of Darius, he
directed his might against the Greeks. In 490 BCE, Darius dispatched a fleet
of ships to land his army at Marathon, on the Greek mainland, just a day's

march from Athens. A small Greek army marched bravely out to meet the Persians, but it seemed certain that the Greeks would be slaughtered, Athens destroyed, and the idea of democracy extinguished.

The Greeks, however, believed that just as every citizen should vote, every citizen should fight. Each Athenian citizen owned his own bronze armor, broad wooden shield, and long iron-tipped spear. The Greeks were veteran warriors (mostly from fighting with each other), and very proud of their skill in battle. Their army was small, but it was made up of people defending their homes and their freedom, while the Persian invaders had been conscripted from many nations and were just obeying orders – and also lacked the fine armor of the Athenians. The armies met on a narrow plain below the hills of Marathon, where the Persian cavalry could not easily maneuver their horses to charge. The Greek spearmen sheltered themselves from the rain of Persian arrows by locking their broad shields together over their heads. Then the Athenian general Miltiades led his men forward against the mass of Persian soldiers. The Greeks were far outnumbered, but their long spears and armor gave them the advantage. The Persians were killed in thousands, and the survivors turned to flee in their ships. The Greeks had defeated the army of the king of the world.

THE DROWNED CITY OF HELIKE

In the winter of 373 BCE, the Greek city of Helike was preserved in a strange and tragic way. It was struck by an earthquake and tsunami, and sank beneath the sea. For years after, its ruins could be seen below the waves – indeed, a statue of Poseidon, god of the sea and god of earthquakes, stood tall enough to snag fishing-nets. But the shifting sands of the ocean slowly covered the lost city, and Helike became just a memory. In 2001 it was rediscovered – along with a nearby town that had suffered the same fate, two thousand years earlier.

Xerxes, the son of Darius and the grandson of Cyrus the Great, came to Greece in 480 BCE to finish what his father had begun. His army was even larger than his father's had been. The finest warriors of the Greek city of Sparta tried to stop Xerxes at a narrow pass called Thermopylae — and every one of them died there. This time Athens could not be saved. Soldiers and civilians alike fled from the city, and Xerxes burned it to the ground. Soon after, however, the united fleets of the Greek cities attacked the navy of the Persians in the narrow channel at Salamis, almost within sight of the burning city. As Xerxes himself watched from a nearby hillside, the Greek warships destroyed his navy. Xerxes went home to Persia, and Greece remained free.

The years that followed the Persian wars were Greece's Golden Age. Confident that their armies and navies could defeat all enemies, the Greeks lost their awe of the mighty empire of the east. They dismissed anyone who did not speak Greek as a "barbarian," because other languages sounded like "bar-bar-bar" to them. Greek cities, particularly Athens, became centers of art and education and culture. In rebuilding their city after Xerxes destroyed it, the Athenians built a temple to Athena, goddess of war and wisdom. High atop the Acropolis, the sacred hill in the heart of Athens, they built the Parthenon, one of the most beautiful buildings of all time, as a symbol of the glory of Greece. Sculptors like Phidias, one of the designers of the Parthenon, carved lifelike marble sculptures with such skill that, even

today, we know what many famous ancient Greeks actually looked like.

The love of debate and argument that went with Athenian democracy encouraged both philosophy and literature. Thinkers and writers who flourished in Greece's Golden Age are still admired and studied today: Socrates the philosopher, Herodotus the "father of history" (he wrote the story of Greece's war with Persia), and the brilliant playwrights Aeschylus, Sophocles, and Euripides. Our modern Olympic Games are inspired by athletic competitions that the Greek city of Olympia held for hundreds of years.

This Golden Age did not last long. Athens began new wars against its Greek neighbors, including a life-and-death struggle against Sparta, once its ally, now its rival. The wars devastated many Greek cities and left the people poorer and demoralized. About a century after the peak of the glory of Athens, Alexander the Great – king of Macedon, in the north of Greece – seized control of Greece. Alexander had been educated by Aristotle, one of the wisest Greek philosophers, but Alexander was more interested in the power of the Greek armies than in earnest debates about philosophy.

As soon as he made himself master of Greece, Alexander marched out to overthrow the Persian Empire. He defeated the Persians, and in a few years he ruled an empire that stretched from Egypt to India. It was said that he wept because there were no more worlds for him to conquer. But Alexander died of illness just before his thirty-third birthday, and his empire began to crumble. Meanwhile, the leadership of the Western world – and the idea of democracy – was passing to a certain city in Italy.

The Age of Rome

Tramp, tramp, tramp, tramp – the thunder of ten thousand feet shook the earth. You could hear a Roman legion long before you saw it: five thousand soldiers marching as one, their armor gleaming, their weapons perfectly aligned. The legions had made Rome, once just a village in central Italy, into the master of the Western world. In Spain, Britain, North Africa, and Palestine, no fighting force could stand against their superbly organized strength and discipline. But the feet of this legion were carrying it toward Rome, not away to defend some distant frontier or subdue a rebellious province. The Roman republic was falling into civil war. The Roman Empire was about to be born.

According to legend, the city was founded by Romulus and Remus, two orphaned brothers who were raised by a wolf and grew up to build a city on seven hills above the Tiber River. The people of Rome believed that had happened in the year 753 BCE — Year One of their calendar. About the time when the Greek cities were defending their democracy against the Persian Empire, the leading families of Rome decided that they would serve no more god-kings. Instead, the city would be governed by a senate of men from aristocratic families and an assembly representing all freeborn Roman men. As Rome expanded its power, the peoples it came to control were invited to become Roman citizens as well. The Romans were inventing what they called in Latin (their language) a *res publica* ("public thing"), a republic. The Roman people would rule themselves. All Roman citizens, no matter where they lived or who they were, would obey the same laws and be protected by the strength of the legions.

The Romans borrowed the best ideas of Greek culture. Philosophers, sculptors, architects, poets, and scientists flourished, and Roman lawmakers created codes of law that still influence the laws of many European nations today. Meanwhile, Rome's legions kept conquering more territory. As Greece declined, Rome took over all of Italy. After a long war with the rival city of Carthage, on the coast of North Africa, Rome's fleets commanded most of the Mediterranean Sea. Rome's governors, backed by the legions, took control of the territories all around its shores: Spain, North Africa, Egypt, the Middle East, and Greece. Rome grew wealthier as the generals who conquered new provinces sent slaves and plunder back to Rome and became heroes to the people there.

About 50 BCE, the most popular and successful of the conquering generals was Julius Caesar. Caesar came from one of Rome's old ruling families. He had been a senator and had held Rome's highest offices. He had proven himself a brilliant general, winning wars wherever Rome sent him. When he conquered France (*Veni, vidi, vici*, he said: "I came, I saw, I conquered"), he brought the power of Rome all the way to the Atlantic Ocean. He even invaded Britain, then a wild, unknown island far from civilization. Caesar was loved by his soldiers and he was popular with the people of Rome, but the senate of Rome feared his growing power and how he might use it. To prevent ambitious generals from using their armies to overthrow the republic, Rome forbade any general to bring his legions into Italy. Caesar defied the law and marched on Rome itself. Civil war broke out. By the end of it, the republic had collapsed. Caesar, victorious as usual, promised to restore the republic – eventually. But he ruled as the dictator of Rome.

CLEOPATRA

Despite all those military campaigns, Julius Caesar found time to romance Queen Cleopatra (69–30 BCE). We don't know if Egypt's famous queen was truly beautiful, but she must have been fascinating and ambitious. Married at seventeen to her younger brother and co-ruler, she led a revolt against him and took over the kingdom, with some help from Caesar. She followed Caesar back to Rome and apparently bore him a son. When Caesar was murdered, she returned to Egypt and married the rebellious Roman commander Mark Antony, probably hoping to win more power for Egypt. But the Roman navy defeated Antony and Cleopatra in a sea battle, and Antony killed himself by falling on his sword. According to legend, Cleopatra used a deadly snake to end her life.

As master of Rome, Julius Caesar had many accomplishments. He even revised the calendar. Roman astronomers knew their calendar did not measure the year precisely. The scientists proposed a new calendar, using a "leap year" – an extra day every fourth year – so the calendar year would match their observations of the sun. Caesar imposed the new calendar upon Rome's empire, and he included in it a new month named for himself: July. Almost 1,600 years after Caesar, a few small changes were made to this "Julian calendar" to make the calendar even more precise, but ancient Romans would recognize our modern calendar.

No matter what Caesar could achieve for Rome, many senators hated his dictatorial rule. They longed to restore the republic – and their own power over it. In

March of 44 BCE, a group of senators met Caesar in the senate building, where his bodyguards were not allowed to go. Led by his former friend Brutus, they handed him a petition and then, when his hands were occupied with it, they drew knives and stabbed him to death.

With the dictator dead at their feet, the conspirators hoped to restore the republic. Instead, they got an empire. After another civil war, Caesar's brilliant young nephew Octavian took power. He adopted the name "Augustus Caesar" and became the first emperor of Rome. All later Roman emperors would also call themselves Caesar.

Augustus came to power in war and civil strife, but he launched a long period called the Pax Romana (Roman peace). No rival could challenge Rome's domination of the known world, and no Roman could challenge the rule of the caesars. The emperor and his heirs built spectacular temples, stadiums, theaters, and public buildings that made Rome one of the most magnificent cities ever seen. Romans said that Augustus had found Rome a city of wood and left it one of marble. Almost a million people lived in or around the city. It and the other great cities of the Roman Empire were the first in history to have such benefits as running water piped into private homes.

Rome had an enormous influence on European history, and world history too. Centuries after the fall of the Roman Empire, kings of Germany

THE COLOSSEUM

Almost fifty thousand spectators could crowd into the four stories of Rome's Colosseum, to watch plays, contests, and duels between professional fighters. (The loser was usually killed.) Famous battles were re-enacted – even sea battles, with boats sailing on water flooding the arena. But the Colosseum also saw horrible cruelty, when prisoners were thrown into the ring with lions and other wild animals. Some of the prisoners were early Christians, and their only crime was their religion.

were called "kaiser" and kings of Russia were called "czar" – both words came from "caesar." Many of Europe's main cities were founded as Roman forts, and Roman architecture, even in ruins, is still a magnificent sight in many of them. No nation today speaks Latin, but most European languages borrow from it, and students still read the classics of Roman literature and philosophy.

The idea of the Roman republic – that all citizens were equal before the law and could share in governing Rome – had failed. Imperial Rome resembled other empires around the world. The caesars were like pharaohs or shahs, surrounded by luxury and corruption. Ambitious men learned that the best way to become emperor was to kill the reigning emperor, and as the years passed, brutal emperors came and went in quick succession. The discipline and loyalty of the legions began to crumble. Invaders from the north and west, peoples the Romans had dismissed as barbarian hordes, began to overrun Rome's distant provinces.

Constantine, who became the Roman emperor in 306 CE, decided in 320 CE to move his capital away from Rome to the city of Byzantium, which he renamed Constantinople (today it is Istanbul, in Turkey). From then on, there were two empires – the one in the west, ruled from Rome, and the eastern one, based in Constantinople. The western empire gradually crumbled, but the Byzantine empire of the east would survive for another thousand years. There was another great change introduced by Constantine. He became Christian, and the new religion of Christianity became the religion of both empires, east and west. Over the centuries, Christianity would become the religion of most of Europe, and it would long outlast Rome's empire.

As one weak emperor after another came to power in Rome, only to be deposed or murdered by a rival who soon suffered the same fate, Rome became unable to defend its borders. The trade and plunder of conquest that had made it so wealthy ceased to flow, and invading tribes called Goths, Vandals, and Huns poured across the frontiers. The Vandals established their own kingdoms in Spain and North Africa. When Rome did not give them all they wanted, they attacked Rome itself. Attila the Hun, the leader of a horde of nomads from the plains of central Asia, was called the "Scourge of God" for the way he destroyed Christian churches and slaughtered their congregations all across Europe. When the Huns invaded Italy from the north, terrified citizens sought refuge on a cluster of swampy islands on the east coast — founding the island city of Venice.

As Rome's empire collapsed and faded, civilizations continue to thrive and prosper in China, the Islamic Middle East, and Central and South America. But from the point of view of Europeans, the centuries that followed the collapse of the Roman Empire were the "Dark Ages." Learning declined. Cities crumbled. Across Europe, people scraped a hard living from the earth in the shadow of ruined temples and engineering works they were no longer able to build. Art, architecture, and science were glories of the past, and so were the Roman ideas of law and government. Europeans learned that history does not always progress from a lower stage to a higher one; sometimes, societies fall back into poverty and savagery. Slowly, over centuries, the people of Europe would have to pull themselves out of the darkness.

POMPEII AND HERCULANEUM

In 79 CE, the residents of Pompeii and Herculaneum enjoyed a fine view of Italy's scenic Mount Vesuvius. But then the volcanic mountain erupted, spewing poison gas and debris. Thousands of people were caught in a deathtrap, and buried under a deep layer of ash and cinders for over 1,600 years. For the citizens it was an unspeakable disaster. For later generations, though, the well-preserved towns — the streets and squares, the shops and houses with their furnishings, the wall paintings and statues — are a fascinating glimpse back into Roman times.

CHAPTER SIX

A PENINSULA WEST of ASIA

We call Europe a continent. But on a map of the world it looks more like a peninsula, a bulge on the west of Asia. In the last thousand years, however, this small part of the world has had more influence on the shape of world history than all the larger continents. It was European people who drew most of the maps, so when they decided Europe was a continent, it was hard to disagree.

On Christmas Day in the year 800 CE, a king named Charlemagne knelt in St. Peter's Basilica in Rome before Pope Leo III, the leader of the Christian church. (The popes have lived in Rome since the time when the Roman Empire was at its height.) Pope Leo placed a crown on Charlemagne's head and declared him "Emperor of the Romans." It was as if the pope dreamed that this tall, strong warrior king could bring back the lost glory of the Roman Empire.

Emperor Charlemagne lived simply, like his warrior ancestors, but his court was a famous center of learning and literature.

In Charlemagne's time, many Europeans knew they were poorer, weaker, and altogether less magnificent than the long-ago Romans whose ruins they could still see about them. Once, a Roman governor in Britain and one in Palestine had enforced the same laws in the same language and served the same senate or emperor in Rome. But in Charlemagne's time, Europeans were divided into many small, battling kingdoms or tribes. They had no common language and no shared code of law, and few of them traveled far from their birthplace, except perhaps to make war on their neighbors. No European society could match the art or architecture of Roman times.

But another title given to Charlemagne pointed toward the future: "Father of Europe." Slowly, the people of Europe would pull themselves up and prepare to discover the world.

Charlemagne came from a people called the Franks. They had been one of the northern European warrior tribes preying on the frontiers of the Roman Empire as it crumbled. With the empire gone, the Franks had settled along the banks of the Rhine River and built their own kingdoms. Gradually they had spread their authority across what is now France (even the name "France" comes from the Franks), Germany, and northern Italy. Charlemagne became the first ruler in centuries to control most of Western Europe in a single kingdom, from his palace at Aachen, in western Germany. He had earned the name "Charlemagne," Charles the Great. (He was "Charles" in the emerging language of French. In German he was "Karl," and in Latin, still used by priests and scholars, he was "Carolus.")

Great or not, Charlemagne could not unite all of Europe, for the Franks or anyone else — not for very long. He could not even unite his family. His sons all wanted pieces of his kingdom for themselves, and eventually Charlemagne's realm was divided among them. His heirs included the first king of France, the founders of several German monarchies, and kings in northern Italy as well. So, in one sense at least, he was indeed the "Father of Europe."

One force that was beginning to bring Europe together was the Christian Church. Most Europeans in the old lands of the Roman Empire were Christians, and many of the invading peoples, like Charlemagne's Frankish ancestors, became Christians as they settled in Europe.

Priests and missionaries continued to spread Christianity to the tribes and peoples on the edges of Europe. Saint Patrick, who is said to have brought Christianity to Ireland, lived not long after Attila the Hun, in the late 400s. In Ukraine, in Eastern Europe, Christianity became the official religion in 988. Not until 1000, when King Olaf of Norway was baptized, did the Christian god begin to replace the fierce old gods of the Norse warriors of Scandinavia. Latin, the language of the Christian Church and of a few learned scholars, was Europe's only common language, and across Europe monks and nuns kept learning alive in the books they copied by hand, and the sacred music they played and sang. All of Europe's oldest universities began as church schools around Christian cathedrals.

Feudal Times

As invading peoples like the Franks settled across Europe, converted to Christianity, and became farmers, their tribes became more complex societies, each with its own territory and ruler. Europe grew into a continent of rival kingdoms and principalities where people's lives were shaped by a system called "feudalism." Under feudalism, there were only three kinds of people. *Those who fought* were the knights, dukes, counts, princes, and kings, the aristocratic families. *Those who prayed* were the bishops, priests, monks, and nuns – a powerful

group in a devoutly Christian world. Everyone else was *those who labored* – the peasants, the farm families who tilled the soil, raised the crops, and tended the animals. In a feudal society, farmers could never own their land. They had to share their produce to support the aristocrats, who governed and protected the land, and the clergy, who prayed to God to protect his people.

Feudalism provided Europe with mighty castles and colorful knights in armor, proud to test their fighting ability in tournaments or on crusade, and with monasteries, abbeys, and spectacular cathedrals whose soaring roofs and glowing stained-glass windows proclaimed the majesty of God and the power of the Christian Church. But Europe had lost the brave idea of ancient Greece and Rome that citizens could have a share in how they were governed. In the feudal system, everyone, high or low, had his or her place, and was expected to stay in it. That didn't mean that kings were absolutely powerful. Everyone looked up to someone and down on someone else, in a chain that linked them all together. Just as the lord in his castle depended on the peasant farmers to support him, the king depended on the lords. The king had to take care of his lords just as the lords had to take care of the peasants. But it would be a long time before the common people of Europe had a voice in decisions and lawmaking, as the citizens of Greece and Rome had had so long before.

By this time, Christian Europe faced a great rival: the religion of Islam, started in the 600s by the Prophet Muhammad in the deserts of Arabia. The caliph (Islamic monarch) ruled a vast empire, with millions of people from western Africa to India, from his capital city of Damascus (now in Syria). Islam was also pushing into Europe. When Muslim armies captured Constantinople in 1453, they brought an end to the Byzantine half of the Roman Empire, founded by the Emperor Constantine more than a thousand years before. Constantinople became an Islamic city, the capital of the Ottoman Empire, which came to rule much of the Islamic world.

Wars and Crusades

Way back in the early 700s, Muslim forces had swept westward across North Africa, crossed the Strait of Gibraltar, conquered Spain, and moved on into France. In 732, Charlemagne's grandfather, Charles Martel, had confronted the Muslim governor of Spain, Abdul Rahman al-Ghafiqi, on a battlefield in central France. After a desperate battle the Christians defeated the Muslims, and Abdul Rahman was killed. Charles Martel's victory helped preserve Christianity as Europe's principal religion, and also helped make the Franks the greatest power in Western Europe. The Muslims retreated back across the Pyrenees mountains into Spain. Not long afterwards, the reign of one caliph over the entire Islamic realm collapsed. While Muslims fought among themselves over a new caliph, Christians slowly began to reconquer Spain.

But Christian Europe did not simply defend itself against the Muslims. It launched its own offensive: the Crusades, a centuries-long quest to regain the region where Jesus had lived and died. Christians had lost contact with this "Holy Land" as Muslims came to dominate the Middle East. In 1095, Pope Urban II began preaching that the Holy Land had to be restored to Christianity, and that Europe's Christians had a duty to win it back. In France, Germany, Spain, and England, princes and knights "took the cross" and promised to fight for their faith. Tens of thousands of ordinary people joined a "People's Crusade" led by a preacher named Peter the Hermit, walking from Western Europe toward Jerusalem.

Few people in Europe knew just how far away the Holy Land was, or how fiercely people all along the route would defend themselves. Most of the peasants who joined the People's Crusade were slaughtered long before they reached the Holy Land, many of them by fellow Christians. The knights and warriors of the crusader army were more successful. They reached the Holy Land, captured Jerusalem, and established a Christian kingdom there, an isolated outpost of Europe in the midst of the

Islamic world. Crusader knights built massive castles across the Holy Land to defend their conquests, and they remained there for almost a century.

In 1187 the great Muslim general Saladin (Salah ad-Din) united the Muslim lands surrounding the kingdom of Jerusalem and prepared to destroy the Christian invaders. First he laid siege to the crusader castle at Tiberius. The French knight Guy of Lusignan, king of Jerusalem, marched his forces out of their stronghold to save Tiberius — just as Saladin had planned. Before the crusaders could reach Tiberius, Saladin's armies surrounded them on a hillside called the Horns of Hattin. On a hot dry day in July 1187, baking in their heavy armor and gasping for water, the crusader armies were cut to pieces by Saladin's warriors. Most of the Christian knights and princes were killed or captured. The popes organized more crusades, but the Christians never rebuilt their foothold in the Holy Land.

Life — and Death

While kings and crusaders fought in the Middle East, people in Europe got on with living and farming. Life changed very slowly for most of them. Children inherited their parents' farms and went on planting the same crops and raising the same livestock. As the population grew, Europe became crowded. Farmers expanded their fields and pastures from the fertile valleys up into the hills. On the edge of the North Sea, the Dutch people built tall dikes to keep out the sea along their low-lying coastline, while they pumped out the water to create new land.

But Europe's population did not always grow. Sometimes new diseases play a greater role in history than kings or warriors. People encounter unfamiliar germs, or suffer an infestation of flea-bitten rats — and suddenly they are struck by a plague of some highly infectious disease. In the 1340s, a thousand years after the collapse of Rome's mighty empire, a plague erupted somewhere in Central Asia. In India and China it killed millions, but Asia had suffered plagues before, and many people had some immunity to this disease. In 1347, however, traders fleeing homeward to escape the epidemic brought the plague to Italy. It was completely new in Europe. It raged across the continent like wildfire, from Italy to Germany to France to Britain, north to Norway — even to faraway Iceland. It was called the Black Death.

FERMENTED SHARK

Icelanders have little land for farming, and live mostly on fish. One traditional dish is *hakarl*, made from the basking shark, a big shark that feeds on plankton. The shark meat is poisonous when it's fresh, so the shark is gutted and beheaded and the rest of the body is buried in the sand, with big rocks on top to press out the bodily fluids. After a few months the meat has fermented, and it can be cut up in strips and air-dried and eaten like beef jerky — if you don't mind the fact that it smells like ammonia.

There was no treatment for the Black Death. There was no cure. If you caught the disease, your glands swelled up, you vomited blood, you collapsed, and you were probably dead within days. If you somehow survived, you might find all your family dying around you, and most of your neighbors. If you escaped from a town that was filling up with dead, you carried the plague with you and spread it to new victims. Most of the community could be wiped out in a few horrible days, until too few people were left to bury the dead, let alone milk the cows or tend the crops. In a few years, a third of all the people in Europe had died. It seemed as if the world was coming to an end.

The plague kept coming back, spreading despair and panic as well as disease and death. But a century after the worst of the Black Death, life in Europe was in some ways better. In overcrowded lands, poor people who had survived the plague could leave their stony fields high up in the hills and move down to the fertile valleys, where the fields and orchards would produce as much food as ever, with fewer mouths to eat it. In the south of France, it was said, wheat was so abundant that for the first time in centuries even the peasants could afford to eat soft white bread instead of cheap, coarse loaves. With a shortage of people, Europeans now had more goods than they needed, and they began to trade more aggressively. It was a good time to be a merchant, a banker, or a sea captain in the trading cities of the continent. Goods were moving, money was flowing. Towns began to thrive again.

Europe had never been the largest or most populated continent. It had not been one of the early centers of agriculture, civilization, and learning. But it turned out that starting late provided many advantages. Europe had a good climate for agriculture, and all kinds of crops and animals that had been domesticated elsewhere grew happily in European fields. Its many long rivers and its extended shoreline along the Mediterranean and the Atlantic encouraged sailing and shipping, both within and around the continent. Sturdy little merchant ships plied the coasts and waterways, carrying wheat from the Polish plains, wool from the fields of England, ironwork from Spain, timber from Scandinavia. Far to the south, the seaport of Venice developed prosperous trade routes to the eastern Mediterranean. Venice became the banker of Europe, lending and investing wherever trade flourished and there was money to be made. Meanwhile, Amsterdam became a center of the trade along the seacoast, while fishing fleets from Holland,

England, and France ventured into the North Sea in search of codfish, gradually pushing their voyages farther and farther across the ocean.

Europe was starting to rediscover art and science. Cathedral schools grew into universities at Padua in Italy, Paris in France, Oxford in England, and Heidelberg in Germany. The wisdom of the Greeks and Romans was valued once again, and European artists took new inspiration from the achievements of the Romans and Greeks. Michelangelo stretched out flat on his back on high wooden scaffolding to paint a vast mural on the ceiling of St. Peter's Basilica in Rome. Leonardo da Vinci captured the mysterious smile on a young Italian woman named Lisa (Leonardo, a poor boy, would have called her "Mona Lisa," "Miss Lisa," out of respect).

At first, Europe's scholars and thinkers called this explosion of knowledge and art the Renaissance, a "rebirth" of the knowledge of the ancient Greeks and Romans. But in fact Europe was creating something entirely new. It was not only rediscovering its past; it was also coming into contact with the rest of the world. Shah Cyrus of ancient Persia had believed he ruled the world. The Roman caesars had made the same boast. Yet those civilizations had known almost nothing of China (though fashionable Roman women loved the mysterious silks that came from there). Now Europe was beginning to forge connections with the Far East.

World Travelers

By this time, China was by far the largest and richest and oldest civilization in the world. In the years between Charlemagne and the Crusades, the vast Chinese empire had been ruled by the Tang and Sung dynasties. During their mostly peaceful rule, China had grown steadily. So had its rice paddies, until in many places the entire landscape was an endless green expanse of rice. China's population had doubled, from about fifty million to about a hundred million – far more than Europe, and all united under a single emperor — and yet China was still growing all the rice it needed, and still avoiding the farming collapses that had struck early agricultural societies in the Middle East, Mayan Mexico, Central America, and elsewhere. For many centuries, Chinese people probably enjoyed the highest standard of living of any large region in the world.

China also had the largest cities in the world. Xi'an — the capital under Shi Huangdi, the first emperor, and again under the Tang dynasty of emperors almost a thousand years later — may have had as many as three million people. China had the most advanced science and technology, and literature and other arts flourished. China and a few of its neighbors were the only places where people had learned to cultivate the silkworm. A single silkworm, held captive and fed on mulberry leaves, can spin half a mile (roughly a kilometer) of silk thread in a few days. Although the techniques for tending silkworms and making beautiful fabrics from their thread were already thousands of years old, Chinese emperors were determined to keep them secret. As a result, Xi'an had become one end of a remarkable trade route called the Silk Road, which ran all the way from China, across the mountains of central Asia, to the Middle East and the Mediterranean. By the 1200s, Venice was doing a huge business in Chinese silk. A family called the Polos were merchants there. They knew as much as almost anyone in Europe about the riches of China, and they wanted to know more.

In 1271, seventeen-year-old Marco Polo traveled all the way to the court of the emperor of China in Beijing, with his father and his uncle. They were presented to the Mongol warrior Kublai Khan, who had just over-thrown the previous Chinese dynasty and made himself emperor. Kublai Khan welcomed his visitors, sent messages to the pope in Rome, and permitted the Polos to learn much about his land. The manufacture of silk was only one of the marvelous things they saw. The Chinese had been the first people in the world to develop papermaking and printing. All the learning of China could be printed in paper books and even in newspapers,

THE PRINTED WORD

About a thousand years ago, the Chinese learned to carve writing and pictures onto wooden blocks, backwards, and press the blocks against ink and then against paper. This "block printing" let them make many copies of a page. But carving the block was a big job, and every page needed a new block. By 1500, Europeans would have a much faster system: making separate letters, and rearranging this "movable type" to print different pages. This would let them produce mountains of books. (The Chinese had thought of using movable type, but their language used thousands of different characters, so it wasn't really practical.)

at a time when the only books in Europe were painstakingly handwritten on sheets of parchment or vellum (made from animal skins). Chinese pottery was so advanced that Europeans called all fine porcelain "china" – as we still do. The Polos watched fabulous displays of fireworks, for the Chinese had invented gunpowder long before it was known in Europe, and they used it for fireworks as well as for rockets and other weapons.

Marco Polo spent nearly twenty years in China before returning home along the Silk Road. It is even said that the Polos brought the recipe for making pasta from China to Italy – but that seems to be no more than a legend.

87

Many other inventions and discoveries that were first developed in China came to Europe through the Islamic world. Islam had spread from the Middle East into India and China, and some Chinese went on pilgrimages to Mecca, in present-day Saudi Arabia, as all devout Muslims were expected to do at least once in their lives. Because the Islamic world now reached so far beyond its homeland in Arabia, many Muslim scholars and travelers saw much more of the world than Christian Europeans could.

Some years after the Polos went to China, a Moroccan scholar named Ibn Batuta made his pilgrimage to Mecca. Then he traveled on, visiting Muslim kingdoms in East Africa, along the coast of the Indian Ocean. Later he went to India, which was then ruled by Muslim emperors, sailed to the islands of Southeast Asia, and carried on to China. After returning home to Morocco, Ibn Batuta journeyed south across the Sahara desert deep into Africa. As he traveled, he wrote detailed accounts of the people he met and the routes he took.

Most of these places remained unknown to Europeans until the works of Muslim travelers and geographers like Ibn Batuta became available. Many of the great mathematical and philosophical works of the ancient Greeks reached Europe from the libraries of the Islamic Middle East. Similarly, Europeans seem to have learned many scientific advances first developed in China, including the navigational compass, papermaking, and the secret of gunpowder, from Muslim merchants and scientists.

The Chinese were great travelers themselves, for a time. Between 1405 and 1433, the Chinese emperor sent his admiral Zheng He on voyages of exploration. Zheng He was able to lead a fleet of more than a hundred sailing vessels, with a crew of thousands, not only along the coasts of China but down through Southeast Asia to India, and across the Indian Ocean to the east coast of Africa. He wrote of sailing among "huge waves like mountains rising in the sky" on the way to "barbarian lands hidden far away." Among the treasures he brought back to China were a giraffe and zebras for the emperor's zoo.

MARCO POLO IBN BATUTA ZHENG HE

Zheng He's voyages expanded China's knowledge of the world, and he brought home marvelous treasures and stories. But China was more a land empire than a seagoing one, and the Chinese had almost everything they needed in China. In the 1430s the empire was caught up in wars and internal strife. After Zheng He died at sea, the emperor called his fleets home, and no more were sent out to sail the world's oceans. Chinese sea captains continued to trade in Southeast Asia and India, but the Chinese gave up their opportunity to explore the world.

No one told the Europeans to stop exploring. Even in Charlemagne's day, Norse sailors from Scandinavia were venturing into the ocean in an open boat called a *knarr*, or longship. Their fighting sailors, called Vikings, had terrorized the coasts of Europe for centuries. Many had settled on lands they had seized in Britain, Ireland, and France. But other Norse adventurers sailed boldly west into the North Atlantic. They settled the uninhabited island called Iceland about 874 CE, and then moved on to Greenland. Around the year 1000, they even reached the coasts of North America. Leif Ericson, son of the first colonizer of Greenland, sailed to a country he called Vinland and wintered there. A few other

Norse adventurers also traveled to North America. But none stayed very long; the native Americans they met did not make them welcome. The Norse soon retreated, and the story of their discovery of America was lost for hundreds of years.

By the 1400s, Europe had kings and governments strong enough and wealthy enough to attempt bold campaigns of exploration and conquest.

L'ANSE AUX MEADOWS

For a short time, around 1000 CE, the Vikings had a small village of cabins and workshops on the island of Newfoundland, in eastern Canada. They seem to have explored the coast and done a little trading with the native people. In 1960 the remains of the ancient village (now known as L'Anse aux Meadows) were discovered, along with tools and other remnants – evidence of perhaps the first European settlement in North America.

There were traders willing to gamble their money on risky new ventures, sailors ready to test their skills in new waters, and soldiers eager for new worlds to conquer. Portuguese and Spanish sailors were venturing into the Atlantic, and down the west coast of Africa.

Humans, of course, have always been a traveling, trading, exploring species. But few took to ocean voyaging as enthusiastically as the Europeans, and their explorations and conquests would change the world forever. Fifty thousand years ago, humankind had begun migrating from eastern Africa and spreading out to find new homes, not only in Africa and Asia, but all over the world: from southern Australia to northern Europe, from Alaska to the southern tip of South America. As they spread out, they had eventually become separate and remote from each other, divided by skin color, by language, by religion, by climate and way of life, by tradition and history, and above all by geography. Even the best-educated Europeans and Chinese, those who had studied science and knew that the world was round, had no idea that the American continents and all the peoples in them existed. The Americas had their own complex civilizations, their scientists and traders and sailors, but they knew nothing of the people on other continents.

It was time for the peoples of the world to rediscover each other. The process of bringing them together would last for centuries, and it would often be brutal and dangerous. Many of the first European explorers would die trying to find and conquer new territories. Countless millions of people in the territories they had come to find would die, or would be conquered, enslaved, robbed, and exploited.

It all began on October 12, 1492.

CHAPTER SEVEN

EXPLORERS *and* COLONIES

Imagine the riverside near Seville, Spain, in August 1492. See that merchant pausing for a moment on the quayside – in that crowd with the child and her nurse, some clerks from the king's customs house, a line of nuns on their way to the cathedral, and a few beggars asking for coins? They are watching three small ships under the command of Christopher Columbus drop down the river toward the Atlantic Ocean. It is no secret: the *Santa María*, the *Niña*, and the *Pinta* are leaving on a voyage of exploration. But where are they going? Señor Columbus says that this time he is not going along the Spanish coast, or east into the familiar waters of the Mediterranean Sea. He is going to strike out westward, into the wild and uncharted Atlantic Ocean.

Explorers like Columbus set out in small, frail wooden ships loaded with fresh water, food, and weapons, as well as horses, cows, pigs, and chickens. There wasn't much room for the crew.

Most people who watched Columbus leaving Spain that day would have known that his ships were in no danger of falling off the edge of the world. Educated people knew the world was round. But no one knew where Columbus was going. He did not know himself. When they headed west, Columbus and his crew were sailing off the map. Columbus believed that, since the world was round, all the riches of the Far East must lie somewhere out there in the west, far beyond the horizon. But in 1492 no one had ever gone all that way and returned.

ISABELLA I OF SPAIN

Isabella's half-brother had been King of Castile. When he died, she and her husband, Ferdinand of Aragon, had fought a civil war to win his throne. Ruling their lands together, they had unified Spain, building roads, maintaining law and order, and driving the Muslims out of southern Spain. Fiercely Catholic, Isabella (1451–1504 CE) was cruel to non-Catholics in those days of savage religious wars. But she is mostly remembered because a persistent sailor implored her to finance a bold exploration. She refused three times but finally agreed, and gave Christopher Columbus the money for his historic voyage.

If that same crowd – the same merchants and nuns and children – had gathered again at the harbor near Seville just thirty years later, they could have watched the ship *Victoria* return to port, battered and worn and with her surviving crew on the edge of starvation. *Victoria* had sailed from Spain in 1519, heading southwest, and had continued right around the world. When she limped back home in 1522, the mystery of what lay beyond the horizon had been solved, but the wonders had only increased.

World against World

By the time the *Victoria* and four other ships set out, the captain, Ferdinand Magellan, knew that Columbus had not found his way to the Far East. On October 12, 1492, Columbus had found the Americas, a "new world" lying between Europe and Asia. Columbus had shown that European ships could survive on the open oceans and come safely home again, and European sailors soon exploded across the oceans of the world. Fishing fleets and whalers found their way across the North Atlantic to a place John Cabot named "New Found Land" in 1497. Portuguese sailors had already ventured south to the bottom of Africa and named its southern tip the cape of *boa esperança*, Cape of Good Hope. Now they continued across the Indian Ocean to India, learning from (and making war upon) the Arab and Indian fleets that already plied that ocean. Where Columbus had hoped for a western sea-passage to the rich trade of Asia, the Portuguese opened up a southeast passage around Africa. By the 1520s, Europeans using the southeastern route had opened permanent trading posts in the Spice Islands (Moluccas) of Southeast Asia, halfway around the world.

Ferdinand Magellan was determined to find a new route, south around the bottom of the Americas and then west to China and the Spice Islands. One of the first things he discovered was how immense the world was. Columbus had crossed the Atlantic to where he thought China ought to be, explored a corner of the "new world," and returned home to Europe in barely six months. Six months out from Spain, Magellan's ships were still feeling their way down the long coast of South America. They had been away over a year before they reached the southern tip of the continent. They emerged from the passage there – now named the Strait of Magellan – and became the first Europeans to sail the Pacific Ocean. But their voyage was far from over. It took them longer than Columbus's entire voyage to get across the Pacific, and they nearly starved. The ocean seemed endless. The men ran out of food and had to boil their shoes, and the ships' rigging, to get a little nourishment. Many found their teeth falling out and their joints swelling. They had discovered scurvy, a disease caused by lack of vitamin C.

At last, Magellan's fleet landed in the Philippine Islands, north of the Spice Islands and not far from China. There, Magellan was killed by native warriors. His crew sailed on, weaving their way through the islands and channels of Southeast Asia. They crossed the Indian Ocean, rounded the Cape of Good Hope, and sailed north through the Atlantic. Finally *Victoria*, the only surviving ship of Magellan's fleet of five, returned to Spain. The crew had been nearly three years away.

It would take another 250 years before the coasts of Australia and Antarctica and some of the northwest coast of North America were added to the map. But between Columbus's departure from Spain in 1492 and the return of Magellan's ship in 1522, the world had been reunited. Suddenly it was possible for Europeans to travel to Asia or America. People from those places could be found in Europe, although usually, at first, as slaves or captives to be shown off. After fifty thousand years, humans once again belonged to one world. For the first time ever, geographers could draw maps of almost all the continents, and of the oceans between them – even if those maps were rough or just plain wrong. Philosophers considered these new continents, and pondered. Were the people there truly human? Where had they come from? In travelers' tales, the seas were full of monsters and the lands were prowled by strange beasts. Who knew what giants or witches, or even supernatural forces, might lurk beyond the oceans? How exotic and mysterious the world had become!

Conquistadors

In 1519, Hernán Cortés landed on the coast of Mexico with a few other Spanish soldiers. They had not come to draw maps or carry home tall tales.

They were hungry for riches and the glory of conquest. They marched inland and besieged the Aztec city of Tenochtitlán and its emperor, Montezuma. Montezuma was a powerful and ruthless prince whose fierce armies had conquered all their neighbors. Tenochtitlán, a glittering city of towers, palaces, and pyramids on islands in the middle of Lake Texcoco, was one of the largest and most beautiful cities in the world. Aztec nobles wore magnificent robes and were covered in jewelry of gold and jade. "These buildings rising from the water, all made of stone, seemed like an enchanted vision. Our soldiers asked whether it was not all a dream," wrote one of Cortés's men. Cortés saw only plunder.

EARLY "VOICEMAIL"

We take instant communication (phone calls, text messaging) for granted, but how did people manage before they were invented? The Incas of South America didn't even have writing, but messages traveled long distances by relays of couriers. Each runner memorized the information, ran one section of the distance, and passed the message to the next runner. The runners carried weapons to fight off anyone who tried to stop them, and conch-shell horns they could blow to warn the next runner to get ready. In Europe, when writing existed but most people still couldn't read, town criers walked through the streets and shouted out the day's news.

97

The Aztecs were brave fighters, veterans of many wars, and there were thousands of them. Great battles were fought, and both sides suffered terrible slaughter. Each time they took a Spanish prisoner, the Aztecs rushed him to the top of the main pyramid of Tenochtitlán and ripped out his heart as an offering to the war god Huitzilopochtli. With his small army overwhelmed, Cortés retreated from the city. But the Aztecs had never seen horses before, let alone fighting men charging at them on horseback. They had never seen metal armor, guns, or gunpowder. Now the Spanish stood back and killed the Aztec warriors from a distance. Eventually, with the help of many nations that the Aztecs had previously conquered, Cortés returned to defeat Tenochtitlán and destroy most of the city. The Aztec Empire became a Spanish colony. Treasure ships began sailing across the Atlantic, taking the riches of the New World to the Spanish king. Cortés saw no value in anything that could not be turned into money. Whole libraries of scientific and literary knowledge were destroyed. The Spanish took over the land and forced the surviving people to farm it for them. Priests and missionaries built cathedrals upon the ruins of Aztec temples. European Christians were once again launching a crusade – this time, to destroy the religions of the new worlds they encountered and to establish the Christian religion around the world.

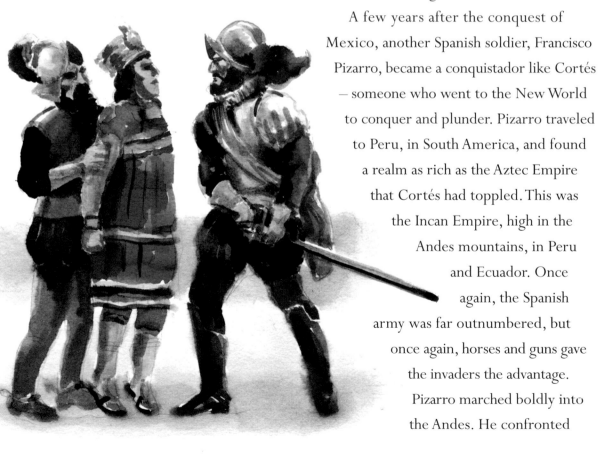

A few years after the conquest of Mexico, another Spanish soldier, Francisco Pizarro, became a conquistador like Cortés – someone who went to the New World to conquer and plunder. Pizarro traveled to Peru, in South America, and found a realm as rich as the Aztec Empire that Cortés had toppled. This was the Incan Empire, high in the Andes mountains, in Peru and Ecuador. Once again, the Spanish army was far outnumbered, but once again, horses and guns gave the invaders the advantage. Pizarro marched boldly into the Andes. He confronted

Atahualpa, the emperor, imprisoned him, destroyed his army, and set about plundering his treasures. Pizarro demanded that the Incas fill a room with gold to buy Atahualpa's freedom, but when they delivered the gold, he had the emperor killed. The wealth of the Incas was sent off to enrich Spain.

MACHU PICCHU

Before the days of the Incas, some civilization in Peru built a settlement way up in the Andes, in the mist between two peaks. Around the 1400s, the Incas took over the city and improved it, building temples and altars and living quarters and staircases. Because land was scarce, they grew crops on narrow steps like Chinese rice paddies. After the conquistadors defeated the Incan Empire, local people remembered the "city in the sky" but it was unknown to the rest of the world – until 1911, when an archeologist searching for another Incan city was led to this magnificent site.

This kind of conquest happened over and over again. With their ships and their guns, the Europeans smashed or defeated almost every kingdom they came up against. Most of Mexico and Central and South America became colonies of Spain – except Brazil, where the Portuguese took control. The Dutch founded valuable colonies in the Spice Islands and at the southern tip of Africa, a stopping point on the route east. The British gained a foothold in India; eventually they would control most of that subcontinent.

In many parts of the world, small numbers of Europeans came to rule much larger native populations. But some areas of the New World became colonies settled by growing numbers of English, French, Spanish, or other Europeans. In time, the English-speaking and French-speaking colonists who set up communities in North America outnumbered the original peoples, the "First Nations." Later, in Australia and New Zealand,

European immigrants came to outnumber the original peoples there. In much of South America, in the Philippine Islands, and in the Dutch colonies of Southeast Asia, European settlers never outnumbered the original inhabitants, but they made themselves the rulers and forced the original inhabitants to become their servants, or to die.

Death Goes Exploring

Europeans were not the only new arrivals in many parts of the world. Germs and bacteria were migrating too. Atahualpa was emperor of the Incas because an epidemic had killed many thousands of people, including the previous emperor. Nearly everywhere they went, but particularly in the Americas, the Europeans brought terrible epidemics of disease.

In 1492, the rich, fertile Mississippi Valley of what is now the United States was home to many prosperous cities surrounded by vast cornfields. The cornfields kept the people well fed. They traded north for furs, west for buffalo pelts, south for dried fish and bright, decorative shells. The rulers of these large cities defended them with earthwork fortifications, and adorned the cities with pyramids and ramps made of smoothed and beaten earth. Yet just a hundred years later, when European explorers began to venture inland in North America, all they found in the Mississippi Valley were small bands of hunters and gatherers. The cornfields were abandoned. The cities were in ruins, their earthwork fortifications now mounds of earth overgrown by weeds. Who were the "Mound Builders" who had peopled these ruined cities, the explorers wondered, and what had become of them?

Early in the 1600s, a French explorer, Samuel de Champlain, explored what is today the Atlantic coast of Canada. Everywhere he went, he found grassy clearings by the shore. Once the villages of the Mi'kmaq nation had stood here, but Champlain found the clearings quiet and deserted. (They would soon be filled with settlers and traders from France.) "Once we were as numerous as the hairs on your head," one of the surviving Mi'kmaq told Champlain. "Since you came among us, we are much fewer."

Where were the people? They were dead, dead of diseases they had never known before Europeans came to their shores. Europeans, Africans, and Asians had been in contact with each other for many thousands of years, and they had been exchanging diseases and germs. Occasionally a new disease, like the Black Death of the 1300s, had ravaged those continents, but the people had built up some immunity to more common germs. (Tropical diseases they were not accustomed to, like yellow fever and malaria, would slow their penetration of Africa and Southeast Asia.) The people of the Americas, however, had been isolated from the rest of the world for ten thousand years, and they had never encountered many old-world diseases. These diseases spread rapidly in the years after Columbus's arrival. They were likely the worst cycle of epidemics the world has ever seen, much more deadly than Europe's Black Death. Probably nine-tenths of all the people living in the American continents when Europeans began arriving died of these unfamiliar diseases. Within a century, only a small fraction of the American population remained. In Australia and other places long isolated from the rest of the world, the cycle of disease and devastation was much the same.

And diseases were not the only hitchhikers on the ships of the Europeans. Animals and plants also had a chance to colonize the rest of the world. Horses had been unknown in the Americas, but after the Europeans brought some horses with them, many American peoples learned to raise and ride them. The Cheyenne, the Sioux, the Blackfoot, and other warrior cultures of the North American plains all rose to greatness as horseback nations, and were soon sweeping across the grasslands the way the ancient Scythians and Mongols had done in central Asia. Pigs were another European import to the Americas; they soon became wild. Rats (and their fleas) came too, hiding in the dark corners of European vessels, then scampering across new islands and continents.

There were no dandelions and no ragweed in the Americas until they came with the Europeans. The same was true of many fruit trees. Apples seem to have been native to the high valleys of Kazakhstan, in central Asia. They had been cultivated in Europe many centuries earlier, and now they came to North America. Europeans brought with them many crops they liked to eat, like wheat, and they also started growing valuable crops from tropical areas, like coffee and sugar cane.

THE CLIFF TOWN OF MESA VERDE

In Colorado, in the western United States, a plateau rises high above the surrounding valley. About 600 CE, the Anasazi people carved homes into multi-level hollows in the steep cliffs inside the plateau. The homes had open-air courtyards, with rooms of brick and sandstone built behind, and people reached them by rock-climbing, or by ladders and carved rock staircases. They lived by hunting, and by farming corn, beans, and squash. Around 1200 the Anasazi left their homes for some reason, and the town – we call it Mesa Verde, "Green Plateau" – was lost until cowboys noticed it a hundred years ago.

New Crops, New Trade Routes

Plants were also sent from the Americas back to Europe. Corn had been unknown to Europeans before Spanish explorers discovered that people in the Americas depended upon it. Rice, the staple food of millions of people in Asia for ten thousand years, was barely known in Europe before the days of great voyages, but it became familiar all over the world. Potatoes and tomatoes were also introduced to Europe from the Americas. Early explorers were amazed at how native Americans took smoke into their mouths, but soon the smoking of American-grown tobacco became a European craze.

All these new foods and new products led to an explosion of world trade. Christopher Columbus had set out to find a faster route to the spices, silks, porcelains, and other treasures of the Far East. The conquistadors had been lured by the chance to conquer empires laden with gold. The merchants who followed also wanted codfish from Newfoundland, and a thousand other products, to fill the holds of their ocean-going freighters.

Coffee was first cultivated in the African nation of Ethiopia, but much of Europe's coffee was soon being grown in the colonies in the Americas. Cotton, native to India and Africa, also became an important American crop. Sugar cane was originally from India, but Caribbean islands were soon covered with cane plantations. Even ordinary Europeans were developing a taste for all these novelties: tea with sugar, clothing made of comfortable cottons, tobacco to smoke. The more Europe wanted all these products, the more it needed colonies to produce them.

But who would grow all those crops in the new plantations in Brazil and the West Indies and South Carolina? Native Americans were dying by millions from epidemics of unfamiliar diseases. European laborers and convicts sent to do back-breaking work in the hot, fever-ridden climates

KOPI LUWAK

In the 1600s, coffee was still a novelty in Europe. Now, of course, we have endless varieties, including Kopi Luwak ("Coffee from Civets.") Palm civets – grey, catlike animals – live in the jungles of Indonesia and eat the ripe red berries of coffee trees. The hard coffee beans inside the berries pass through the civet's digestive system and end up in civet poop on the jungle floor. Workers collect the beans and scrub them, and they are sold as the world's most expensive coffee beans, treasured for their special chocolaty flavor.

of the New World died in great numbers too. Plantation owners soon turned to Africa, and to slave labor. They began to buy slaves in vast numbers, to labor in the Americas.

Slavery

"There was nothing to be heard but rattling of chains, smacking of whips, and the groans and cries of our fellow men." A thirteen-year-old boy from Ghana named Ottabah Cugoano had been seized by slavers. He was chained in the dark, reeking hold of a slave ship with dozens of other unhappy captives and sent across the Atlantic, never to see his home again. Ottabah Cugoano found himself in a slave market on the spice-growing island of Grenada, in the West Indies. He might have lived and died there, but an English merchant purchased him and took him back to England, where the boy gained his freedom. One of the very rare slaves to escape from bondage, he learned to read and write and eventually published the story of his life.

From 1500 until about 1850, more Africans crossed the Atlantic than Europeans. Probably twelve million were enslaved and sent on the cruel and often deadly voyage, to a short, brutal life in the New World. As slaves on plantations, they tended sugar, cotton, tobacco, coffee, and other crops. From Brazil to the Caribbean islands, and north to the southern states of the future United States, the labor of slaves fueled the growth of European colonies. Once more, the population of the world was mixing.

Europe did not conquer Africa, but all along the West African coast there were European "castles," forts, and trading posts where slave traders bought Africans and sent them off to the New World. Africa was poor, with many people but few goods, and warring nations found they could make themselves richer by selling their fellow Africans. As captives were dragged away to hard labor and rapid death on the plantations that were making Europe rich, Africa remained poor.

Wars of Religion, Wars of Freedom

Year after year, treasure fleets sailed from Mexico and Central America, bringing the gold and silver and emeralds of the New World to fill the Spanish king's treasury. Spain spent its new wealth trying to expand its European empire to match the empire it had won in America and in Asia.

In late July of 1588, less than a hundred years after Christopher Columbus made his famous voyage, King Philip II of Spain sent forth another fleet of ships – the "Invincible Armada." It was going not to discover new worlds, but to invade and conquer England. The Armada, 130 vessels strong, approached the English Channel in a roaring gale. The plan was that the Armada would seize control of the Channel and destroy the English fleet, and then a Spanish army would cross the narrowest part of the Channel in boats and swiftly conquer England for the glory of Spain. With England fallen, Spain's rebellious colonists in Holland would abandon their resistance. France would yield to Spain's leadership. King Philip of Spain's great ambition would be fulfilled: Spain would control Europe as surely as it controlled Mexico, Peru, and the islands of the Caribbean.

Just outside London, Queen Elizabeth I gathered her own army. Elizabeth was a remarkable woman. She never married, and she ruled England on her own in a time when such power was considered the right of men, not women. "I have the body of a weak and feeble woman, but I have the heart and stomach of a king," she told her soldiers. They roared back their support for her, but as it turned out, the soldiers did not have to fight. Along the Channel coast, Elizabeth's captains harried the Armada every day. The English ships proved themselves faster and better armed than the Spanish ones. Barely a week after entering the Channel, the Armada's ships were smashed by gunfire, short of supplies, and running aground. Finally, the Spanish fleet fled the Channel and made a desperate run for home, sailing right around the British Isles, north of Scotland and down the rugged coast of Ireland. In the storms of autumn, many were sunk or wrecked. Only a shadow of the Invincible Armada – battered and broken – struggled back to Spanish harbors. England was safe.

Why were Spain and England fighting? For power, of course – but not just power. Something new was dividing Europe: religion. The tension between the Catholic Church and Protestant reformers was tearing Europe apart.

Europe had been Christian since the days of the Roman Empire, and Christianity's hold had been strengthened by Europe's long wars against the Islamic forces of North Africa and the Middle East. The pope governed the Roman Catholic Church from Rome, and was also the leader of Christian Europe, expecting the allegiance of kings and princes across the continent.

In 1517, about the time Spanish conquistadors were launching their first attacks in Mexico, a Catholic monk named Martin Luther nailed a statement of protest to the door of a church in Germany. This was the start of the "Protestant Reformation." Protestants rejected the teachings of the Catholic Church, and declared that they needed no pope and no bishops. With prayer and the Bible, they said, they could shape their religion themselves. Very rapidly, Europe split into Catholic and Protestant zones. There were people of passionate religious faith and deep piety on both sides, but Catholics and Protestants fought each other as bitterly as Christians had battled Muslims in the Crusades. Victims were

imprisoned, tortured, even burned at the
stake. Fierce religious wars blazed across
Europe for years, leaving devastation
and hatred in their wake.

Elizabeth I was a Protestant
queen in a mostly Protestant country.
Philip II was a fervent Catholic, the
pope's strongest ally. If the Spanish
forces had conquered England, that
might have tipped the scales against
all the Protestant countries and led to
the Catholic domination of Europe.
But England remained free, and the
Protestants continued in their faith
— not only in England and much of
Scotland, but in Holland, many
areas of Germany, Switzerland, and
parts of France. The rest of France,
Italy, much of Germany, and the
empires of Spain and Austria remained loyal to Catholicism and the
pope. Europe grew into a patch-
work of independent nations, rather
than a unified Catholic continent.

In the spring of 1648, European diplomats gathered in a small
German town to put an end to the long struggle. The carnage of the
wars of religion had been horrifying. Much of Germany had been
reduced to a wasteland. All the fighting powers were exhausted and
ready to call a truce, and the diplomats had come to negotiate a peace
treaty. Although they did not know it, they were reinventing Europe as a

continent of many nations, each shaped by geography, by language, by shared religion and history and culture.

Even as the diplomats were negotiating, England was fighting a bitter civil war. The king, Charles I, wanted to be absolute master of his realm. He believed God had chosen him to rule over England. But the idea was growing that a nation belonged to its people. If the English would not listen to a distant pope, why should they bow down to an absolute monarch? England's Parliament demanded a voice in the running of the country. Charles and his Parliament quarreled for years, until Charles finally declared that all Englishmen who were loyal to him must stand with him against Parliament. His war against Parliament failed. In 1649, the English Parliament tried and convicted the king of England for treason. On a cold January day, Charles I knelt by the execution block in London and had his head chopped off.

Eventually the English allowed Charles's son, Charles II, to become king. But never again would any British king or queen rule as an absolute monarch. The British were developing what they proudly called "the rights of Englishmen." A king or queen would continue to reign, but would not rule. He or she would have to accept the advice given by the Parliament, which represented the people. The ancient Greek and Roman idea – that people could participate in their own government – was returning to Europe.

In the next century two more nations would rebel against the rule of a monarch. The first of these revolutions came in the British colonies of North America.

Not all of Europe's colonies had been built by conquistadors and slave laborers. Settlers from Spain, France, Holland, and all the countries of Western Europe had crossed the ocean to settle in the New World – to escape persecution, to seek a better life, or just for adventure. Britain's colonies on the eastern coast of North America were among the most successful. By the mid-1700s they had large cities, busy seaports, and thriving farms. Compared to people in Europe, most of these colonists were well-off, educated, and active in running their own affairs. Many were no longer willing to be ruled by Britain's king or Britain's Parliament.

FROM THEN TO NOW

THE STATUE OF LIBERTY

In 1876, when the United States celebrated its first hundred years of independence, the people of France sent them a dramatic anniversary present. The Statue of Liberty is a symbol of freedom and democracy, showing a woman holding a tablet that represents knowledge. The copper statue, 152 feet (46 meters) tall, was built in France and then taken apart and shipped across the Atlantic in 214 crates. Today, "Lady Liberty" stands in the entrance of New York Harbor, welcoming immigrants to their new home.

In 1776, the colonists threw out their royal governors and signed a declaration of independence. Led by a wealthy plantation owner named George Washington, they fought a successful war to become free of the British Empire, and they founded the United States of America. Some of them thought George Washington should be made king, but it was decided that the United States should be a republic as Rome once had been. "We hold these truths to be self-evident, that all men are created equal," says the opening of the Declaration of Independence. There would be no king. Their leader would be a president, elected by the people and subject to the same laws as everyone else. These were noble ideas, but not noble enough. Many of those who signed the Declaration of Independence were slave owners who had no intention of freeing their slaves, let alone accepting them as equals.

The other revolution was in France, only a few years later. On July 14, 1789, a mob of angry citizens stormed the Bastille, the royal prison at the heart of Paris. They slaughtered its garrison and seized its weapons.

The king of France was still an absolute ruler. At first, the leaders of the revolution imagined that they could control him with an elected parliament like Britain's. They drafted a lofty declaration of "the rights of man," and made "Liberty, Equality, and Fraternity" the slogan of their revolution. They decided to make *everything* new. They changed the date from 1789 to "Year One." They gave new names to the days and months, introduced a new measuring system (the metric system), and decreed that there would be no more dukes or counts or princes; everyone would be a *citoyen*, a citizen of the republic of France. As the symbols of the old, unjust aristocratic regime came crashing down, another great advance in human freedom seemed to be within reach.

THE EIFFEL TOWER

In 1889, France held a "universal exposition" in Paris to mark the hundredth anniversary of the French Revolution. The Eiffel Tower was built of iron, on the bank of the River Seine, as an impressive entrance to the exposition. It's named for its designer, Gustave Eiffel – the man who engineered the Statue of Liberty – and it's 984 feet (300 meters) high. In those days, great iron and steel bridges were being constructed to span rivers and carry trains drawn by steam engines. But although massive ironworks were fashionable, many people thought the tower was a disgusting eyesore. Today, it's the most famous symbol of Paris.

But times were hard in France. The poor people of Paris and the farmers of the countryside were crushed by debt. They bitterly resented the arrogance of the French nobility and the royal family, who lived in luxury and splendor at the magnificent palace of Versailles. The revolution quickly became violent. It was symbolized by the guillotine, a fearsome mechanical blade designed to chop off heads more efficiently than any axe-wielding executioner. King Louis XVI and his family, and then thousands of aristocrats, and then anyone denounced for being "counter-revolutionary," died on the guillotine. After that, the revolutionary leaders began executing each other, in a fierce battle for power that became known as "The Terror." France found itself at war with the monarchies of Europe, and a brilliant young general named Napoleon Bonaparte saw his opportunity. Napoleon's troops took control of Paris and threw the people's representatives out of government. In 1804,

Napoleon declared himself emperor of France.

Napoleon, a poor boy from the Mediterranean island of Corsica who became the most famous person of his time, was one of those extraordinary people who seem to remake history just by being there. He was a brilliant soldier; he seemed to have an instinctive sense of where his enemy's weak point lay and how his troops could take advantage of it. As a result, the armies of France surged across Europe, occupying Italy, Germany, Austria, Spain, and, briefly, even Russia. He supported the arts, rebuilt Paris, and revised all the laws of France. It seemed there was little he could not improve. Yet he was also a tyrant; he shared power in France with no one, and spent almost his whole career at war with most of Europe.

And not only with Europe. The Napoleonic Wars became world wars, fought in the Caribbean Islands and India as well as in Europe, and even drawing in the United States. On the colonial island of Hispaniola in the Caribbean (now Haiti and the Dominican Republic), black slaves on the sugar plantations heard the message "Liberty, Equality, and Fraternity" and decided it should apply to them too. They rose up in revolt against their masters. Led by a former slave, Toussaint L'Ouverture, they won their freedom. Across South America, the Spanish and Portuguese colonies founded on the conquests of Cortés and Pizarro also demanded freedom. Simón Bolívar, a young Venezuelan, became El Libertador, calling for the liberation of the South American countries, and for them to join together in a great democratic federation. Spain's rule in South America did collapse, but the newly free colonies became independent countries (one of them, Bolivia, is named for Bolívar), and most of them were soon controlled by military dictators, not elected governments.

In 1815 Napoleon's good fortune began to run out. A coalition of the great powers of Europe combined against him. Napoleon met the

British army at Waterloo – in Belgium, north of France – and used his artillery, his cavalry, and his infantry. Finally he sent his finest troops, the Imperial Guard, to smash the enemy line. But the Duke of Wellington, the British commander, withstood every attack. By the end of the day the British troops had been joined by their allies. The French lines had crumbled and the reign of Napoleon was finished. The emperor of France surrendered after a few days, and was sent in exile to the remote island of St. Helena, in the South Atlantic, where he died six years later.

France had come through many upheavals, and there were more to come. But the spirit of "Liberty, Equality, and Fraternity" would survive. July 14 – the day that angry mob stormed the prison in Paris – is now Bastille Day, France's national holiday, the day the French republic was born.

CHAPTER EIGHT

The AGE of INDUSTRY

In 1750, Manchester was a small town in northern England. It was an old town; it had got its name from the Romans, who had occupied Britain almost 1,500 years earlier. At nearby places like Lancaster and York, powerful lords had ruled from grand castles, but Manchester had never been that important. The people in the rural areas around town were farmers, mostly sheep farmers. Manchester was known mostly for the woolens and linens that its weavers and spinners made for England and elsewhere.

With the Industrial Revolution, business was booming. These British blacksmiths are working at a forge, probably making another ship's anchor like the one in the foreground.

In the 1700s, prosperous English farmers were finding ways to farm more effectively. They experimented with better plows, with machines for seeding, and with methods of breeding better livestock – "improving" farmers, people called them. Better farming methods allowed each farm to produce more food or raise more animals with the same amount of human effort. Meanwhile, in the town of Manchester, cloth merchants and weavers were seeking similar innovations to make them more efficient. They developed machines that could prepare wool and linen and cotton yarn more quickly, and weave it into fabric faster than by hand.

Around Britain, other new ideas were bubbling up. A young Scottish inventor named James Watt was trying to harness the power of boiling water and the steam it produced. In 1776, he came up with the first really practical steam engine, in which water in a boiler, heated by a coal fire, turned into steam that drove a piston that could run a machine. This was not just some hobby or science project. Watt immediately formed a company to build steam engines and sell them to businesses like the fabric mills of Manchester. Other experimenters began to develop coal mines in the north of England. They could see that in the future coal might not just be heating homes or fueling blacksmiths' forges. It could power furnaces to drive those new steam-powered machines.

Coal and Steam, Filth and Soot

In 1781, England's first steam-powered factory opened in Manchester. It was a cotton mill. With coal-fired steam engines driving fast new machines, the factories of Manchester began producing more cotton cloth, more quickly and more cheaply, than any other place in the world. The town led the world in cotton cloth – even though no one anywhere near cool, damp Manchester grew cotton, which is a subtropical plant. Manchester did not need to grow its own cotton, because conquerors and trading companies and colonists had given Britain access to unlimited supplies. Manchester's raw cotton came from British-controlled India and from the slave plantations of the United States. Even the fact that Manchester was an inland town with no harbor did not matter. Canals linked the town's mills to the coast, and in 1830 the world's first railroad (driven by steam engines) began running between Manchester and the seaport of Liverpool. Because its factories were so efficient, Manchester could export cloth from its mills back to the very places where the cotton

had grown. Soon, ships built of iron and powered by steam engines were replacing the wooden sailing ships that had carried the world's freight for thousands of years. Most of the new steamships were British-made and British-owned.

Manchester, once a weavers' town, became a city of factories. The engine works and machine shops that produced equipment and tools for the cotton mills began supplying machines for many other industries. Manchester had the machines, the steam engines to drive them, and the coal to keep the steam up in them. There was one other requirement: people, more and more people, to work in the factories.

Workers poured into Manchester from the countryside around, and then from farther away. New farm machines meant that fewer farmers could produce more food, so English farming continued to thrive, no matter how many country folk moved into town. Manchester grew teeming and prosperous, but it did not grow beautiful. It was black with soot from the coal fires that drove its mills and factories. It had grown so fast that it did not have proper housing or sewage or schools. Waste from the factories polluted the water. The workers, even young children, put in very long days in the factories for little pay, and they ate and slept in crowded slums where they hardly saw the sun. But while the working people were poor, Manchester and other towns – like Glasgow in Scotland and Birmingham farther south, all now crowded with factories and lined with canals and railroads – were helping Britain emerge as the richest country in the world.

For ten thousand years, wealth and prosperity had come from agriculture. All the great civilizations had been built on the labor of farmers, and in every civilization most people had been farmers, for it took that much of the population to produce the food that supported kings and lords, priests and scholars, merchants and artisans, and soldier and sailors, most of whom were better known and more prosperous than the humble farmers. In the 1700s and 1800s, however, England was exploring a new way of living. With machines and scientific methods, fewer farmers could produce all the food Britain needed – and factory workers could produce goods far beyond anything the old agricultural societies had ever dreamed of.

Industry Takes Over

Ever since the first smiths hammered gold into jewelry and copper into arrowheads, human beings have been a tool-making species. Ever since the first wheels and pulleys, we have been inventors. Ever since we got horses to carry our loads and hoisted sails to push a boat forward, we have tried to harness power other than our own muscles. Some of these discoveries were made by hunting and gathering peoples here and there, many thousands of years ago, through happenstance, or by trial and error over the centuries. As agriculture developed, the rise of cities and trade and literacy increased the pace of discovery and invention. Thinkers and inventors began to ponder the chemistry of metals, the physics of movement, the mathematics of architecture.

Every civilization made some new contribution to science and technology. As trade and written communications became more extensive, ideas – from algebra to gunpowder – slowly spread around the world. In many places, prosperous civilizations supported places of learning: Confucian academies in China, schools of philosophy in ancient Athens, Islamic madrasahs in the Middle East (the first university degrees ever granted were in madrasahs), monasteries and universities in Europe. China, one of the world's oldest and longest-enduring civilizations, was the first source of many remarkable inventions. With its lush fields of rice keeping the population fed, and its trade in silks and china and other luxuries bringing in wealth, China was probably the richest country in the world for centuries. Now, though, it was Europe that was finding the path to industry.

Europe had been growing richer and more confident as new ships and new weapons let it conquer much of the globe. Europeans benefited from the scientific knowledge of ancient Rome and Greece, and borrowed what they could from Chinese and Arab scholars. Their schools and universities supported the spread of knowledge – about gravity, about how the human body worked, about chemistry. In the 1500s and early 1600s, the astronomers Copernicus and Galileo shocked the world with their theory that the earth rotated around the sun, instead of being the center of everything. In the 1800s, the British scientist Charles Darwin put forward his theory of evolution. He declared that human beings were related to apes, instead of being created in God's image. Both these theories demanded that people change their whole view of life and the universe.

Meanwhile, merchants and inventors were searching for practical but less earth-shaking discoveries: new tools, new processes, new ways to harness energy to drive machines. Not far from Manchester, Darwin's relatives the Wedgwoods experimented with pottery. They became the first in Britain to learn to mass-produce fine china, and other makers quickly imitated them. Suddenly it was Britain, not China, selling china to the world.

Other countries raced to imitate and improve on what the British were doing. In Essen, Germany, a wealthy family of ironworkers, the Krupps, saw Britain's advances in iron-making and steel-making. The Ruhr Valley around Essen was well supplied with iron ore and with coal mines, and soon the Krupp factories in Essen were producing iron and steel in huge quantities. They were famous for their cannons, but the Krupp motto was "We make everything." Before long, tens of thousands of Germans were streaming from the countryside to factory cities and mining towns along the Ruhr Valley. Other factories found many different ways to use Essen's steel. An inventor named Rudolf Diesel had designed an engine that ran on a new fuel derived from oil, and he got the Krupps to build it for him. Now the steam engine had a rival: small, portable engines that ran on gasoline or diesel fuel.

In the United States, coal was abundant in the hills of western Pennsylvania, and in the mid-1800s the Pennsylvania town of Pittsburgh began to grow into an American version of Manchester or Essen. By then, railroad trains driven by steam locomotives were pushing out across the United States. The first American transcontinental railroad linked the east with California in 1869. A Scottish immigrant named Andrew Carnegie built some of the world's largest steel mills in Pittsburgh, to supply steel for all the railroads binding the United States together.

The thousands of laborers who put in ten hours a day in Pittsburgh's roaring, dirty, often dangerous mills were as poor and overworked as their fellow workers in Manchester. Like laborers elsewhere, they formed unions to fight for better working conditions and better pay. In 1892, a bitter strike broke out at Carnegie Steel's works near Pittsburgh. Many workers were killed by Carnegie's private security forces, and the union was smashed. Carnegie went on to become one of the world's richest men. Later in life, he used his fortune to build public libraries all over North America.

Henry Ford Moves to Detroit

Henry Ford was born on a farm in Michigan, in the United States, in 1863, but he was never much of a farmer. Mostly, he loved to tinker with machinery. When his father gave him a pocket watch, Henry took it to pieces to see how it worked; that was the kind of challenge that interested him. When he was about sixteen he drifted to the nearby city of Detroit, where he worked with steam engines and sawmills. Sometimes he had to go back to the farm to earn money, but what he really wanted to do was build an automobile. He wasn't alone. All over the world, tinkerers like Henry Ford were putting engines on wheels and trying to make them run. In Detroit alone, Louis Chevrolet, Walter Chrysler, David Buick, and the Dodge brothers were just some of the men turning carriage-building shops into automobile workshops.

DOTS AND DASHES

Although other people were working on similar inventions, an American named Samuel Morse generally gets the credit for inventing the telegraph. In 1844, he sent a message from Washington to Baltimore over an electrical wire, in the form of short and long bursts of electricity. The signals of "Morse Code" are called dots and dashes, pronounced "dit" and "dah." For example, Morse Code for the letter D is long-short-short, or "dah-dit-dit." Telegrams remained useful well into the 1900s, even after telephones were in common use.

It was a good time to be a tinkerer. All through the 1800s, a flood of inventions had been changing life, at least in the developed world. Railroads and steamships made it possible for goods and people to move much farther and faster than ever before. The telegraph – the first successful transatlantic line was laid beneath the Atlantic Ocean in the 1860s – and then the telephone let news and information pass almost instantly around the world. Electrical power had been developed in the early 1800s, and by the second half of the century electric lighting and electric heating were becoming available. In 1895, generating stations driven by the water falling over Niagara Falls began producing the first hydroelectric power for transmission over what seemed then to be a long distance: all the way to the nearby city of Buffalo, New York. Soon, cities much more distant from power dams and waterfalls could be lit and heated by hydroelectricity. Meanwhile, the first oil wells were developed at Oil Springs in Canada and Titusville in the United States, in 1859. At first, most oil was refined into kerosene for burning in lamps, but soon oil would find a new market: providing power for automobiles.

HOLD THE PHONE!

In 1876, Alexander Graham Bell managed to speak a sentence over a telephone wire. The first phone messages were hard to hear, but technology improved and telephones became popular. Towns began installing switchboards, with operators who connected callers to the desired numbers (and sometimes eavesdropped on the calls!) Telephone wires were strung between towns and across countries. Families could talk to relatives a thousand miles away to pass on urgent news or just to say, "Happy birthday!" The world was suddenly much smaller.

When Henry Ford first took over a carriage-maker's shop in Detroit, in 1896, the automobile was still strange and rare. He called his first auto a "horseless carriage," and it looked like one. Driving was an expensive hobby in those days, and cars were used mostly for racing and stunts. Inventors like Ford built them one or two at a time, and anyone who owned one had to be adventurous and mechanical.

In 1908, Ford developed the car that would change that. He called it the Model T. It was simple, rugged, not very expensive, and big enough to hold the whole family. Unlike lots of other autos of its time, it had doors and a roof and a windshield to make it practical and comfortable. Ford said his new car would be cheap enough that almost any working family could own one, and enjoy "hours of pleasure in God's great open spaces."

Henry Ford was not the first to build automobiles, and Model Ts were never the best cars around. It was the way he built them that made the difference. Other car builders were craftsmen, creating their cars mostly by hand. But soon after he designed the Model T, Ford and his engineers designed a factory that could build cars by the thousand. All the Model T parts coming into Ford's new factory were standard, and they could all be organized along the sides of a slow-moving "assembly line." A crane hoisted the iron frame of the Model T onto one end of the assembly line. As it was slowly carried forward, hundreds (later thousands) of workers along the sides each installed one part or completed one small task. When all the pieces had been added, a complete Model T rolled off the end of the line. It sounds simple, but Ford's assembly lines produced a new Model T every three minutes – about eight times faster than his older methods of building cars. And faster meant cheaper.

At last there was a car cheap enough and reliable enough for almost every family – first around Detroit, then across the United States, then in other countries too. To make his car even cheaper, Ford stopped offering the original range of colors; customers could have any color they liked, he said, so long as it was black. In a few years, Ford was producing 300,000 Model T cars a year. In twenty years of production, his company sold more than 15 million Model Ts. Henry Ford would never have to go back to the farm again. In fact, he bought the farmhouse where he was born and put it in his museum near Detroit.

Until competitors copied Ford's assembly-line system and began to offer cars with new styles and colors, Model Ts outnumbered all other cars on American roads put together. Because Ford had decided to put the steering wheel on the left side of the Model T (on some of his earlier cars, the steering wheel was in the center), this became standard in North America. By the 1920s, America was on wheels – and most of those wheels were on black Model Ts.

But cars could not run without roads, traffic lights, driving rules, gas stations, and repair shops. Car factories could not operate unless there were iron and steel producers, and parts makers, and suppliers of rubber tires, and power to run the factories and machinery. When the first oil wells were drilled, not long before, oil products like kerosene and gasoline had been used mostly for lamps (replacing whale oil), but now the automobile created an enormous new market for gasoline. The more industrial progress there was, the more new inventions were needed.

Between about 1900 and the 1920s, the United States went from having a handful of hobby cars to having millions of trucks and cars. The pace of North American life had begun to shift from the speed of a horse-drawn wagon on a country road to the speed of traffic roaring along a superhighway. Ten thousand years before, farming had created a whole new way for human beings to live. Now the Industrial Age was drawing people from farms to cities, and changing human life again. Indeed, it was changing the planet – and in time it would reach into space.

Life on the Farm

Do you know a story like this? A family lives in the city, but when summer comes, they jump in the car to visit Grandma and Grandpa on the farm. The kids play with the animals, run through the fields, swim in the creek. They sleep in a big feather bed in the attic and discover a little bit about country living, before waving goodbye and returning home.

No law says that grandparents must live in the country when the kids and their parents live in the city. But stories like this used to be common in movies and books and on television, and they rang true for a lot of kids. Older generations stayed in the country, where they had been born; younger generations found work in the expanding cities.

In 1900, most people all over the world were farmers. Some sold their crops or animals to customers in faraway cities, even across the ocean. Others farmed mostly to feed themselves, and many lived very plain and simple lives, wearing homespun clothing, eating the wheat or rice or corn or sorghum they grew, buying just a few luxuries, lighting a candle or lantern for a little while before going to bed soon after dark. Often they could not read or write, and they rarely traveled beyond their own neighborhood. They might be dominated by landowners who claimed a share of their produce as rent. Their lives might be ruled by all-powerful kings, generals, or colonial governors, as their parents' and grandparents' had been. Millions of people all over the world had no say in how their country was run, though their sons and brothers might be obliged to fight in its wars.

In 1900, farmers in many places around the world still worked by hand, aided only by animals and a few ancient technologies like windmills and watermills. In China, India, Africa, South America, and parts of Europe, they still walked through their fields behind a horse or ox pulling a simple plow. They cast their seeds by hand, and in the fall the whole family pitched in to harvest the crops with long-handled scythes, to thresh the good grain from the dry chaff, and to bundle up the straw for animal food. But industrialization was changing that, and the changes spread through nearly all the world during the twentieth century.

Where teams of farmhands had once walked through the fields cutting ripened stalks of grain by hand, a gasoline-powered combine driven by one worker could rumble through in a few minutes, cutting the stalks, separating and storing the grain, and leaving the straw to be tied into bales by another machine. Where cows had been milked by hand for centuries, they were now attached to milking machines. Chemical fertilizers enriched the soil more than animal manure could, so more crops could be grown. "Hybrid" seeds — developed by plant breeders by cross-breeding different varieties — yielded larger, hardier crops. Electricity, which had begun powering street lights and lighting private homes in the cities of Canada and the United States and a few other places in the late 1800s, began to reach the countryside. Gasoline-powered trucks and steam-driven trains and ships carried farm produce farther and more efficiently than wagons and canal barges and sailing ships ever had. Refrigeration preserved spoilable foods during shipment, and factories started canning and, later, freezing foods so that they would travel better and last longer.

With all these improvements, the world did not need nearly as many people to produce food. Wherever industrial farming took hold, a few farmers with a lot of machinery could produce as much as hundreds of farmers working by hand. But if machines replaced most of the people working in the countryside, what were all those extra people going to do? No problem; they could find work in the cities.

In 1900, only about thirteen percent of the world's people lived in cities. At the start of the twenty-first century, fifty percent lived in cities. In the wealthiest, most developed countries, as many as eighty percent are city-dwellers. Even in the poorest societies of India and Africa, there was a great migration from the country to the cities in the second half of the twentieth century. Vast numbers of people left the farm, moved to the city, and only went back to visit Grandma and Grandpa.

City Life

In Detroit and Pittsburgh in the United States, in Toronto and Montreal in Canada, in Manchester and Birmingham in England, in Essen and Frankfurt in Germany – in many places around the world, small towns grew large and prosperous, with smoke-belching factories employing thousands of people to turn out truckloads of manufactured goods. Running these industries was a complicated business. Assembling raw materials, processing them, shipping them, and selling them required workers in offices as well as on the factory floor. Banks sprang up, and insurance companies, department stores, advertising agencies, and services of all kinds. Cities grew every which way.

Industrialization brought more than new tools and new machines. It changed the way people saw the world, and the way societies operated. Back in agricultural times, what mattered most was who owned the land. Most property was owned by aristocrats who lived in big houses and controlled military power, and their vast stretches of land were farmed for them by poorer families. This system could be very unfair, but it had a certain stability. People knew what their position was – what they owed to the ranks above and below them – and all this was unlikely to change.

In this new industrial society, land was much less important. The social position someone was born into was also less important. A poor farmboy like Henry Ford could become wealthy and powerful through his own ingenuity and hard work. Once people found a way to make their first fortune, they could make more and more money, if they were wise in their investments. Those who were clever enough and lucky enough could become fantastically rich.

But in a society where people were responsible for taking care of themselves, what would happen to those who were unable to?

Some people believed that society would find its own balance, that industry would create enough prosperity for everyone. Way back in 1776, in his book *The Wealth of Nations*, a Scottish economist named Adam Smith had written about manufacturers and farmers and merchants competing to buy what they needed as cheaply as they could and to sell what they produced for the highest price they could get. This competition created a "market," wrote Smith. While individuals fought to enrich themselves, the market was like "an invisible hand" keeping everything in balance, pushing everyone to work hard and to be as efficient as possible.

Adam Smith also saw how specialization – in which each worker did one special job – would make production more efficient. A worker making pins all by himself might make just a few pins a day. But if a team of workers could divide up the job and specialize in various parts of it, they might produce thousands of pins a day – particularly if they had machinery to help them. Smith predicted that with specialization, the invisible hand of the market, and the use of new machines and energy sources, people would produce more than ever before, and life would be better than ever before.

Not everyone was so optimistic. Karl Marx, a German philosopher who lived in Britain for many years, observed the dark, crowded, dangerous factories where people often hated their jobs, and the terrible poverty working people suffered in the industrial cities. He argued that the owners of the factories – the "capitalists" – would always exploit the workers if they could. He was sure that, one day, the workers would rise in revolt against the capitalists and introduce socialism, in which all people would be equal and would share the hardships and benefits of their work equally.

But there was another possibility, a middle ground between these two extremes. Ordinary citizens could take more control over the way their society was run. They could even choose the people who ran it. After all, rulers who were elected by the people would have to find ways to keep them happy.

Over the course of the 1800s, slavery was finally abolished, almost everywhere in the Western world. More and more people won the right to vote – first men, then women. They chose who would run their countries, their towns, even their schools. Eventually, some areas started holding plebiscites – votes on specific questions like "Should we build a new bridge?" This was "people power" – *demos-kratos*, democracy – the same idea the ancient Greeks and Romans had had, but including many more people as citizens.

When all those workers had a voice in government, they were able to make important changes in their lives. Perhaps their children should be in school, learning to be responsible, useful citizens, instead of doing dangerous, menial jobs in factories. Perhaps, in a fast-changing world where people might be employed one day and unemployed the next, there should be insurance for those who lost their jobs. Perhaps there should be pensions for people who could no longer work, and healthcare for people who couldn't manage to pay a doctor, and loans for students who couldn't afford to stay in school.

Perhaps there was no need for a bloody revolution to bring social justice. Life might indeed be controlled by an "invisible hand" — but it could be the hand of the citizens themselves.

For Better and for Worse

With all these changes, many people had more freedom and security than ever before. They could choose where to live, what kind of work to do, how to spend their leisure time. They could travel, or have the world brought right to their doors — in a pizza box or a carton of Thai noodles. They had more possessions than ever before — cars, appliances, fancy clothes, toys.

SPIDER FRIES

Some foreign treats have never caught on in the Western world. In Cambodia, people enjoy munching on a-*ping*, furry tarantula spiders the size of the palm of your hand. The spiders are raised as food, fried in oil with a little garlic and salt, and sold as street snacks — chickeny in flavor, crispy on the outside and soft in the middle.

But they had lost something, too. They no longer felt the close connection to nature that their hunter-gatherer ancestors, and even their farmer parents, had enjoyed. Instead of being part of the natural world, they were a burden on it. Forests and plains had been turned first into farmers' fields, and then into highways. Wild animals had become products or pets, or had been driven toward extinction. As the human population grew larger and larger, and took up more space and needed more industry, the planet was damaged. Air and water and land became polluted. Within a few centuries, people burned up huge amounts of energy — electricity, coal, oil — that nature had created over millions of years.

CHAPTER NINE

EUROPE'S WORLD

Who was the most powerful person in the world in 1897? A conquering emperor from an ancient line of kings? An eastern prophet with a new message for the world? One of the new masters of American factories and railroads? No. The most powerful person was a plump, elderly widow living in England. Every day she dressed in black to mourn her husband, who had died more than thirty-five years earlier, and she did her best to keep herself hidden away from the world. Her name was Victoria, and in 1897 she had been Britain's queen for sixty years. To celebrate the sixtieth anniversary of her reign, her Diamond Jubilee, princes, rajahs, chieftains, governors, and prime ministers came from British territories all over the world for a grand procession through the streets of London, to pay homage to the old lady dressed in black.

Queen Victoria reigned for sixty-four years and was called "the grandmother of Europe"; her grandchildren included a German emperor, a Russian czarina (queen), and a Norwegian queen.

The World Colored Red

Victoria did not actually rule Britain. An elected prime minister and government made the decisions. But politicians came and went, and everything they did was done in the name of the queen. By 1897, few people could remember anyone but Queen Victoria wearing the crown. Her Majesty symbolized Britain and the vast British Empire. To the Blackfoot Confederacy of western North America she was the "Great Mother" who had made treaties with them. In India she was the queen-empress who ruled millions of people although she had never set foot in their land. In Africa, her name graced the largest lake and a thundering waterfall a mile (1.6 kilometers) wide. Fleets sailed and armies marched in her name. In forts and government buildings around the globe, her portrait held the place of honor.

The Roman Empire had been gone for about 1,500 years, but schoolkids in Queen Victoria's Britain still learned Latin, the language of the Romans. (Not all kids; many hardly went to school at all, especially if they were girls.) Wealthy British families believed that the language and literature of ancient Rome (and ancient Greece too) were the best preparation for young Britons who would be going out to rule the world. Indeed, many British people thought Britain *was* the new Rome – except that it encircled the whole world, instead of just Europe and the Mediterranean.

One of the Latin phrases that British schoolkids learned was "Pax Britannica," meaning "British peace." After Napoleon's empire came crashing down at the Battle of Waterloo in 1815, there were no more great wars among the nations of Europe for a hundred years. Through all those years the British navy prowled the oceans to enforce the peace, and no nation on earth was strong enough to challenge the British Empire. The smoke-belching factories that had made Britain the first industrial nation had also made it the richest country in the world. "We hold the greatest empire that has ever been," Britons told themselves proudly. On maps of the world the British Empire, colored red, seemed to cover most of the globe. And it was getting larger.

"Dr. Livingstone, I presume?" said the American journalist Henry Stanley in 1871. The famous explorer David Livingstone had been lost in Africa. Now, after ten months of trekking through dangerous, violent country, Stanley had found Livingstone, in a dusty lakeside village near the source of the Nile River. What a great story for his newspaper!

Except that David Livingstone was *not* lost. He had been living among the Africans for years as a missionary, fighting against slavery and trying to "civilize" Africa. He wanted to spend his life among the Africans. He believed that he was helping Britain build a new kind of empire. He was no conqueror like Cortés or Pizarro. He wanted to help the people of Africa, and teach them his Christian religion and the British way of life — so superior, in his mind, to anything in Africa.

During Victoria's time, Europeans began exploring the interior of Africa — its mighty rivers, its inland empires — and taking the message of Christianity everywhere they went. Behind the missionaries and explorers came Britain's armies and colonial governors, as mission stations and trading posts became British colonies. During her reign, Britain took control of more than a third of Africa. British leaders talked of building a railway "from the Cape to Cairo" — from South Africa to the Mediterranean — on British-held territory all the way. Parts of Africa that did not become colonies of Britain were snapped up by rival powers. France and Italy acquired colonies on the Mediterranean coast of northern Africa. Belgium seized the more central Congo. Germany started colonies in southern and eastern Africa. Soon there were almost no independent African states left on the continent. Some Africans got the schooling and "civilization" that David Livingstone intended, but most colonial officials everywhere considered Africa "uncivilized" and in need of European control. They described this control as their responsibility and called it "the white man's burden."

NZINGA M'BANDI

Back in 1623, when the Portuguese were expanding their empire into East Africa, Nzinga M'Bandi (1581–1663) saw that her brother, king of what is now Angola and the Congo, was not strong enough to resist them. Making herself queen and organizing a guerrilla army, she won a peace treaty with Portugal. When Portugal broke that treaty, she went to war again, leading the army herself and letting women serve as soldiers. She ruled for forty years, giving women high positions in her government. Not until she died, in her eighties, were the Portuguese able to seize her land.

The Jewel in the Crown

India has had many civilizations over thousands of years, and many religions; it has been home to Hindus, Buddhists, Jains, and Parsees, among others. In the 900s, Muslims moved into India, and eventually Muslim kings ruled much of the land. In the 1500s, a powerful Muslim dynasty called the Moguls began uniting India into a single empire. Their capital, Delhi, became one of the great cities of the world. In the 1630s, one of the Mogul emperors, Shah Jahan, built the Taj Mahal, often called the most beautiful building in the world, as a memorial to his favorite wife. But even under the Moguls, India was still made up of many peoples with many local rulers. Rajahs (kings), princes, and chiefs all kept their own elegant courts, their private armies, and their elephants and camels.

At first, the British went to India as traders. In 1600 their East India Company began setting up trading posts along the coasts, so that they could buy Indian goods and ship them to the markets of Europe. The trading company sent its own troops to India, to protect its traders and to fight rival companies from France and other European countries, and in time these armies became the most powerful force in India. As the Mogul Empire crumbled, the East India Company became the real master of India, although the British government became more and more involved in controlling the area.

In 1857, the Indian troops of the company rose up in rebellion, seeking to overthrow the foreign invaders. After a brutal conflict, the rebellion was crushed, but Britain then stepped in, took over from the company, and made all of India a British colony. The British called it "the jewel in the crown" of their empire. There were still more than six hundred native kingdoms, but now their rajahs and ranis (queens) ruled in name only. The upper castes (classes) lived in wealth and comfort, lavishly dressed, covered in jewels and gold, dining elegantly and surrounded by magnificent art, while the poorest peasants lived in grim poverty. But the real rulers were the British soldiers, engineers, and administrators — a few thousand European men and women upholding British rule over millions of Indians, all in the name of Victoria, Queen of Great Britain and Empress of India.

137

THE TAJ MAHAL

Shah Jahan's favorite wife was a Persian woman named Mumtaz-i-Mahal, "Jewel of the Palace," and he was devastated when she died. In her honor he built the Taj Mahal, a magnificent white marble mausoleum (tomb building) set among gardens and fountains, and decorated with colored stones like carnelian (red), jasper (green), and lapiz lazuli (blue). One of the patterns on the tomb links red poppies (a symbol of eternal sleep) and blue Persian irises. Now, almost four hundred years later, the shah and his beloved lie together beneath this graceful dome.

The Humiliations of China

For much of the time that Queen Victoria ruled the British Empire, the Chinese Empire was also ruled by a woman, the Empress Dowager Cixi. She seized power when her husband died in 1861 and dominated China until her death in 1908. Women were not supposed to rule in China, so she ruled "from behind the curtain," issuing imperial commands in the name of her son, the emperor. She kept herself even less visible than Queen Victoria, but she was an absolute ruler, not a symbol or a figurehead.

China's story during that era is a sad one. China had long been the richest and most advanced society in the world, and for centuries Europeans had been eager for Chinese silks, teas, ceramics, and other fine goods. By Queen Victoria's time, sea captains and merchants – British, Germans, Portuguese, and others – clustered at the mouth of the Chang (Yangtze) River, and around islands like Hong Kong and nearby Macao. They built European-style settlements on Chinese territory and ran them under European law, as if they were not in China at all.

Although Europe never conquered or colonized the mainland of China, its traders and missionaries reached deep into the interior. When the Empress Dowager tried to control these intruders, European armies and navies attacked. They even invaded and seized her imperial capital city, Beijing – not once but twice.

As European influence grew stronger, the power of the ancient empire crumbled. People rebelled against their empress, causing terrible destruction and loss of life. Despite its glorious past, China had now fallen far behind. As Europe grew prosperous and industrialized, more and more Chinese people became poor farmers, getting by on their rice and other crops.

As their homelands became poor and dominated by Europeans, Indian and Chinese people began emigrating to other parts of the world. Indian laborers went to work in the sugar-cane plantations in places like the faraway island of Trinidad, in the West Indies. Most people in Trinidad were the descendants of Africans brought there to be slaves. Now, the Indian immigrants joined them.

About the same time, Chinese workers were hired to help build railroads in the western United States and Canada. This was desperately hard work, and many died in explosions and rockfalls. But in China, where poverty and hunger were so common, North America was called "the Golden Mountain." It was a place where men could find work and send money home for their families. When the railroads were built, some of those Chinese workers settled in American and Canadian towns, opening shops, laundries, restaurants, and other businesses. They were becoming part of North American society.

Land of the Shoguns

Across from China, on the other side of the Sea of Japan, lay an intensely private, traditional land. Japan had been ruled since 1603 by the powerful Tokugawa family. The Tokugawas were not emperors, but they completely controlled each emperor, and they named one of their own as each emperor's shogun (advisor). For 250 years these Tokugawa shoguns were the actual rulers of Japan, and all that time they strove to keep Japan closed off from the rest of the world. Almost no foreigners were allowed in. Foreign influences, including Christianity, were suppressed. Millions of poor rice farmers were dominated by a military class called "samurai." Once upon a time the samurai had been warriors, but under the iron rule of the shoguns there was no need for war. During the centuries of peace, the samurai prided themselves on their knightly honor and their skill in martial arts, but they rarely fought in actual wars.

As the rest of the world moved forward, many Japanese were unhappy that their land seemed to be frozen in time. There were uprisings among the peasants. Other noble families were jealous of the Tokugawas' power. Foreign traders — especially the Americans, from across the Pacific — wanted the country to allow foreign trade. In 1857 Japan was forced to open up its borders, and the long rule of the shoguns collapsed. A new emperor took the throne, to preside over the modernization of Japan. He was called the Meiji Emperor. He was just fifteen years old.

The Meiji Emperor did open Japan to the world — but not to colonizers rushing in to carve up the country and dominate its trade, the way they were doing in China. Instead, Japan became the first Asian country to imitate the Industrial Revolution of Europe and North America. Japan began to encourage modern science and mass education and business enterprise. It copied and borrowed European technology. At the same time, it defended traditional Japanese culture and discouraged the Christian missionaries who had become so influential in Africa and China. Japan began importing raw materials from the rest of Asia, and manufacturing many products, particularly clothing and fabrics, that it could sell all over the world. It built a modern army and navy and opened banks and stock exchanges. Managers and diplomats switched easily from their traditional kimonos to business suits. Japanese kids took up baseball.

FUGU

The Japanese still cherish many of their traditions, like dining on fugu (pufferfish). Fugu has deadly nerve poison in some of its organs, and it's difficult to cook the fish without poisoning the dish. Local chefs aren't allowed to prepare it unless they are specially trained and licensed in the thirty-step process. Although people die every year from eating poorly cleaned fugu, the dish is highly prized — perhaps because, even when it's prepared correctly, the fish may still hold enough poison to give the diner an exciting prickling feeling.

Japan's new strength shocked the European nations. Their ideas of human equality and human rights still applied mostly to white people. All the leading countries of Europe, and the United States as well, had built empires in which small numbers of white men had almost total power over the lives and homelands of non-whites like Africans and Asians. Many Europeans believed that their wealth and power and civilization proved them superior to people of other "races." So Japan's success – Japan even defeated Russia in a war in 1905 – challenged their confidence that they were better than all other people, and destined to rule over them.

Not all Europeans believed in the superiority of white people. Around the world, the idea that humans should not own humans was gaining strength. Opponents of slavery, called "abolitionists," had long demanded that slavery be banned. A small, bold sect of Christians called The Society of Friends – or "Quakers" – denounced slave-holding as a sin, and other Christians, like David Livingstone, agreed. The British Empire banned the trading of slaves across the Atlantic in 1808, and in the 1830s Britain abolished slavery throughout its empire. Most of the nations of South America and the imperial powers of Europe soon did the same. In the United States, however – where the cry of "liberty" had launched the American Revolution – the fight over slavery was growing more and more bitter.

The War between the States

At the end of June 1863, two armies – one in blue, one in gray – marched to confront each other in the wheatfields and peach orchards around a small town called Gettysburg, in eastern Pennsylvania, in the United States. First the cavalry came galloping toward the town, exchanging a few shots when they met the enemy, then riding back to warn the armies. Up came the regiments of infantry, sweat soaking their thick wool uniforms as they marched along country roads in hot sunshine. Behind them rumbled horse-drawn artillery, supply wagons, medical crews. The generals rode up with their aides and messengers, looking over the ground and directing their men to seize hilltops and other good positions. The troops kept coming until 160,000 men were gathered there. They would fight a terrible battle, until one army was smashed and broken. Thousands would die, and thousands more would be horribly maimed. Yet the soldiers on both sides were Americans. Their country had split apart in a bloody civil war, and the outcome hung on the battle at Gettysburg.

The American Civil War was fought over slavery and freedom. In 1776, the opening words of their Declaration of Independence – "We hold these truths to be self-evident, that all men are created equal" – had been a shocking claim. In those days, nearly all societies were ruled by hereditary leaders who took it for granted that they were superior to the people they ruled. The claim had made the United States, the first large democratic republic in the world, seem like a beacon of freedom.

But not all Americans were equal. Many were not even free. On the plantations of southern states like Virginia and Georgia and Louisiana, black slaves picked the cotton for the mills in England and the northern American states. Slaves tended tobacco and the other crops that helped make the southern states prosperous, and worked as household servants and ladies' maids, and did all kinds of menial labor. White southerners defended slavery as part of their heritage. They knew that their wealth, even the comfort of their homes, depended on the very low-cost labor of slaves.

The northern states were more industrialized and much less dependent on slavery. More and more people there were determined to abolish slavery. They insisted that the promise of the Declaration of Independence must be kept. They publicized the horrors of slavery, helped escaped slaves reach freedom, and campaigned against this shameful oppression.

As the United States continued to expand west, the question flared over each new state — would it be a slave state or a free state? The argument tore the nation apart. In 1861 the slave-holding states "seceded" from the United States and became an independent country, the Confederate States of America.

The northern states — led by their new president, a tall, homely man named Abraham Lincoln — declared that the unity of the nation had to be preserved. The two sides, north and south, slid into a war not just between states, but between friends and relatives. At first, both sides imagined that this war of Americans against Americans would be brief and almost bloodless. Surely the other side would not really fight? But both sides grew more determined as the war went on. Industrial progress gave both sides better rifles and more powerful cannons than in previous wars, and factories to produce plenty of them, and railroad lines to deliver them wherever they were needed. The conflict became a long, horrible war neither side could win.

Two years into the war, the Confederate general Robert E. Lee had come north toward Gettysburg pursuing a bold plan. Battle after battle had been fought in the south, and General Lee had won nearly every one. He and his troops had begun to believe they could never be beaten by the "Yankees" of the north. Now he was leading his men into the heart of the northern states. If the Confederates could win battles on the north's own territory, the north might lose heart and seek peace, and the southerners might get to keep their slaves.

The armies met just south of Gettysburg, and for two days they pounded each other with cavalry charges, barrages of artillery, and other maneuvers. The Union (northern) side held its ground, but the Confederate (southern) side was still confident that its enemy would soon collapse and run. Finally, on the third day, General Lee gathered twelve thousand soldiers into a long line and prepared them to surge across the fields, toward the line of Union troops. Some of his commanders warned him that the men would be mown down before they achieved their goal, but Lee trusted his brave, determined soldiers. The war depended on them. If they could break that line, the northern army would be shattered. If they could just break that line. . . .

The Confederate soldiers charged across the fields into a rain of deadly fire, walking at first, then running, bunching together as bullets and cannonballs plowed their comrades down. Their only hope lay in reaching and breaking the enemy's defenses. One of the Confederate commanders led a handful of men right into the line of Union soldiers, but they got no farther, and the commander was killed along with his men. The great charge faltered to an end. The Confederate survivors began to retreat, helping their wounded friends across a field covered with dead and hideously wounded men. Barely half the Confederate soldiers returned from the charge. General Lee, always a gentleman, thanked them and said that the failure was all his fault, not theirs.

General Lee had to retreat back to the south. Although there were still many battles to fight, the Union began to grind down the resistance of the Confederacy. In the last year of the war, a tenth of the soldiers in the Union forces were African-Americans, carrying the fight for their own freedom into the heart of the land of slavery. Finally, in the spring of 1865 – almost two years after the Battle of Gettysburg – Lee surrendered to the Union forces. The states were united once again, and slavery was abolished throughout the nation. Six hundred thousand people – one American in fifty – had died in the struggle.

A few months after the battle there, President Abraham Lincoln visited Gettysburg to dedicate a cemetery for the thousands of dead. His speech, the "Gettysburg Address," was barely two minutes long, but it became one of history's most famous speeches. In a few sentences, Lincoln declared that the war was being fought to decide whether a new nation "conceived in Liberty, and dedicated to the proposition that all men are created equal" could survive. He said that the outcome of the terrible war must be "a new birth of freedom." Lincoln, however, would not live to see it. Just days after the war ended, an assassin shot him dead while he was watching a play.

Clash of Empires

In the years after the Civil War, the United States grew rapidly. It attracted immigrants from Europe by the million. It built up factories, railroads, and cities, and expanded across the continent toward the Pacific. Cattle ranchers, farmers, and gold miners poured onto the plains and into the western hill country.

Native nations still ruled on the plains. There had been wars between them and the Europeans since the days of the first colonies, and the natives had slowly been pushed west. Now their entire way of life was threatened, and so were the huge herds of buffalo that many of them depended on. The wars between natives and whites — especially the army cavalry — became relentless, with atrocities committed by both sides.

The most famous of the natives' enemies was George Custer. Custer had been a general during the Civil War, when he was only twenty-four. After the war he became a colonel in the cavalry. In 1876, when the army was beginning a massive military campaign against the natives in the territory of Montana, Colonel Custer and over two hundred of his men attacked some Sioux and Cheyenne warriors near Little Bighorn River. But there were more warriors there than Custer had expected, and they were brilliant at fighting from horseback. Among them were heroes like the Sioux war chiefs Crazy Horse and Sitting Bull.

Custer and all his men died at the Battle of Little Bighorn, now remembered as "Custer's Last Stand." But the natives' victory there could not save their way of life. Soon, the buffalo were almost wiped out, and the people themselves were forced to settle on small reservations. Sitting Bull fled to Canada. Crazy Horse was thrown in jail and stabbed to death when he tried to escape.

While all this turmoil was going on in the United States, there were also some changes north of the border. In 1867, the remaining British colonies in North America, which were already largely self-governing, became the nation of Canada — the first colony of European settlers to become an independent nation peacefully and democratically.

Fighting "little wars" against indigenous peoples was one way that European nations built their empires. The United States acquired colonies in the Philippine Islands and in the Caribbean, and it built up one of the most powerful navies in the world. It was not the only nation flexing its muscles and expanding its reach. Many European countries were beginning to challenge the supremacy that the British Empire had held for most of a century. Germany and Italy, long divided into many small, weak states and principalities, became unified nations in the 1860s and 1870s. After Napoleon's defeat, France had been ruled by several kings and by Napoleon's nephew, Napoleon III. In 1870 it became a republic with an elected president. All these rising powers wanted to compete with Britain, first by building colonial empires, and later in Europe itself.

As the nations of Europe expanded the democratic reach of their parliaments, industrial and commercial growth was spreading prosperity more and more widely. More children were going to school, housing was better, medical care was improving. Fewer children died in infancy. When the children grew up, they had a growing range of career choices. And if they didn't like what they found at home, they could emigrate to Canada, the United States, Australia, or elsewhere. Yet even as people's lives seemed to be improving, storm clouds were gathering.

ROTTEN CHEESE

Europe has its share of peculiar dishes. The Italian specialty of *casu marzu* ("rotten cheese") can only be made with the help of cheese flies. The flies lay their eggs on the cheese. When the maggots (larvae) hatch, they burrow into the cheese and release enzymes that break down the fat, giving the cheese a soft creamy texture, a powerful smell, and a rotten taste. Italy has banned the cheese because it's not very safe to eat. Some people make it anyway, and scrape off the wriggling maggots before eating it – or swallow it maggots and all.

In 1906, King Edward VII of Britain, the son of Queen Victoria, proudly launched a mighty new battleship, the *Dreadnought*. Soon after, Kaiser Wilhelm II of Germany watched the launch of his own version of the *Dreadnought*, the *Nassau*. The Meiji Emperor saw the launch of Japan's dreadnought-style battleship, the *Satsuma*. Before long, the United States, France, Austria, and other countries all had their own dreadnoughts. They were a super-weapon, the most spectacular warships ever seen. They were enormous, carrying crews of two thousand or more, yet they were faster than most naval vessels. They were covered with steel armor, and their decks bristled with immense guns that could fire explosive shells at distant ships before they were even visible over the horizon.

Dreadnoughts were expensive, but Europe's military leaders feared that whichever nation launched most of them would rule the seas. They were entering a competition that could leave the winner controlling the whole world. To protect themselves, the various nations began constructing a tangle of alliances: promises that *these* nations would protect and support *those* nations against their common enemies. Although Europe dominated much of the world, it now seemed on the edge of disaster. Any spark could set off an explosion.

The Great War

The spark was struck in June 1914. The heir to the throne of the empire of Austria-Hungary was shot dead while visiting Serbia, a nation suspected of seeking to undermine Austria-Hungary. Thirsting for vengeance, Austria-Hungary declared war. Serbia turned to its ally Russia, and Russia declared war on Austria-Hungary. That brought Austria-Hungary's ally, Germany, into the fight. France took the side of the Russians (Germany was France's traditional rival) and so did Britain and her empire. By August 1914, all of Europe was at war.

"It will all be over by Christmas," people told each other. Who could imagine the world's most advanced civilization throwing away lives, prosperity, and its place in the world? There would be a quick victory, people said confidently, and then peace would return.

It was not over by Christmas. Soon, it was known as "The Great War."

In the last great war Europe had known, Napoleon's armies had thundered over Europe from Portugal to the gates of Moscow. In 1914, many Germans expected that their soldiers would roll quickly into Paris. People in Britain and France looked forward to seeing their armies sweep into Germany and occupy Berlin. But now a new weapon was available: the machine gun. Tended by just a couple of soldiers, it could spew out five hundred bullets a minute. All the European armies had thousands of machine guns. The face of warfare had changed.

The war quickly settled into a blood-drenched stalemate. Soldiers became experts in digging narrow trenches where they could hide from enemy fire, and soon an elaborate network of trenches, tunnels, dugouts, and underground shelters scarred Europe from the English Channel to

Switzerland. Gunfire from both sides plowed up the ground between the trenches, and rain turned the ground to mud. Winter came, and millions of crouching, mud-caked soldiers shivered in the cold, wet trenches, suffering as much from "trench foot" – a horrible disease that rotted their toes – as from enemy fire.

A few got to soar above the mud of the trenches. Orville and Wilbur Wright of the United States had flown the first heavier-than-air powered aircraft in 1903, and now fighter planes and bombers were part of warfare for the first time. Manfred von Richthofen, a German aristocrat, had been raised to be a cavalry officer like his ancestors, but there was no place for horsemen in trench warfare. Richthofen took to the air. He and his squadron flew bright red aircraft that swooped and dived far above the muddy trenches, and he became the most successful pilot of the war, famous on both sides as the "Red Baron." Warfare in the air was more comfortable than trench warfare, but just as dangerous. New fighter pilots lasted about a week, on average. In 1918 the Red Baron was dueling with two young Canadian fliers when he was killed by a machine-gunner on the ground.

At 7:30 a.m. on July 1, 1916, in the Somme, a river valley in northern France, the British and French armies arose from their trench lines to attack the enemy. It was Gettysburg on a vastly larger scale, and the German machine-gunners mowed down the attacking soldiers by the thousands. At mid-morning, word came back to the British lines that the attack was succeeding at a place called Beaumont-Hamel. The Newfoundland Regiment, the lone regiment that Britain's outpost in the North Atlantic had sent to support the war effort, was ordered into "no man's land." But the attack was not succeeding, and the enemy machine-gunners were alert and waiting. The next morning, when the Newfoundland Regiment called the roll, only 68 of the 801 who had attacked reported for duty. On the first morning at the Somme, twenty thousand soldiers were killed among the British forces alone. More than a million would be killed and wounded before the battle wound down in November, and the trench lines had hardly moved.

The war went on like that for more than four years. There was fighting in some of Europe's colonies, but mostly it was fought in Europe. Oddly enough, the costly dreadnoughts that the rival nations had built so feverishly hardly left their ports throughout the conflict. The war was fought mostly by soldiers emerging from their stinking trenches to gain a little ground one week, only to lose it the next week, while their comrades died around them.

At first the United States stayed out of this European war. But German submarines sank a British ocean liner, the *Lusitania*, and over a hundred American passengers died. Then Germany announced that it was increasing its submarine warfare, so that no country's ships would be safe. In 1917, the United States finally joined the war, adding its military might to the cause of Britain and its allies. A year later, Germany and its exhausted allies asked for peace, and the war ground to a halt on November 11, 1918.

The victors said it was a triumph of civilization over barbarity, of liberty over militarism. President Wilson of the United States said it was a "war to end wars." But every European nation had sacrificed a generation of its young men, and much of its wealth as well. Before World War One, it had seemed that Europe was on the verge of controlling the whole world. Its imperial nations were using their new industrial strength to complete the conquests that had begun with Christopher Columbus. After the war, Britain and the other "winners" built up their empires by taking over the colonies of their defeated enemies. They did not yet know that the great destruction Europe had unleashed on itself had undermined its global dominance. As the twentieth century rolled forward, the rest of the world was about to step onto the stage.

CHAPTER TEN

The STORMY TWENTIETH CENTURY

One night in 1893, a young lawyer from India named Mohandas Gandhi was thrown off a train in the British colony of South Africa. The white settlers of South Africa did not like sharing their train compartments with non-Europeans. Gandhi spent the night shivering in a cold railroad station, and what he decided there changed the world.

Twenty years after the end of World War One — "the war to end wars" — a German dictator was taking over Europe, bit by bit. The world was creeping toward another war, even more dreadful than the last one.

In the dark of the night, Gandhi began thinking about the injustice of racism, and how to resist it. He had studied law in England, but he was also a student of the Hindu traditions of his homeland. By combining the Western idea of "civil disobedience" – refusal to obey the law for reasons of conscience – with Eastern teachings of nonviolence, he came up with a philosophy that he called *satyagraha* – "the force of truth." He declared that victims of injustice and racism should *not* respond violently. Instead, they should speak the truth and act on it. Peaceful resistance, he said, was the right way for people to defeat violence directed against them. They should refuse to accept unjust laws and taxes. They should disobey oppressive authorities, even if that meant being put in jail. They should organize themselves to get along without oppressive laws or governments or businesses. *Satyagraha*, Gandhi said, came from strength, not weakness. Decent, righteous people were stronger than those who committed injustices. They could triumph without using the methods of their enemies.

Gandhi lived for years in South Africa, but in 1915 he returned to India and began to work for the freedom of his country, which was still a British colony. Gandhi and his allies began insisting that the British must leave India. They refused to pay British taxes. They refused to buy British-made goods. They defied British laws. Gandhi led mass marches and held hunger strikes, insisting that Indians had the same right to India as British people had to Britain.

As Gandhi became famous and influential all over India, he took to living very simply, more like a traditional Hindu wise man than an English-trained lawyer. He ate no meat, he wore only very simple garments, and he tried to spin cloth every day to demonstrate that Indians could provide for themselves. His simple life and his political cause made him a hero. By the 1930s he was known to the people of India as Mahatma, "great soul."

But Mahatma Gandhi and his cause had not triumphed, in India or anywhere else. All over the world, Europeans ruled non-Europeans. The Great War had weakened the European powers, but they did not intend to give up their authority. Gandhi continued to preach his message of peaceful resistance and of India's freedom. He continued to ask why Indians and other colonized peoples could not govern themselves, why a handful of Europeans ruled in India and Africa and so many other lands. In many parts of the world, however, tyranny was increasing.

Comrade Stalin

For most nations, the Great War ended in 1918. For Russia, it ended in 1917. In every battle, the untrained, badly equipped, underfed soldiers of Czar Nicholas II had been slaughtered by superior German armies. Early in 1917, after a disastrous winter, the Russian army began to fall apart. Regiments refused to fight. Bedraggled, footsore soldiers straggled back home. They had gone forth loyally to do as their czar commanded, but now they blamed him for their sufferings. He had betrayed them. Things had to change.

Czar Nicholas II was a Romanov, and his dynasty had ruled Russia for more than three hundred years. One of his ancestors was Peter the Great, who had been so eager for Russia to learn from more advanced countries that he had once gone in disguise to Holland and worked for months in a shipyard. When he returned, he built Saint Petersburg – a new seaport from which Russia could trade with Europe. Another ancestor was Catherine the Great, who had invited some of Europe's greatest philosophers and artists to her court at Saint Petersburg. As their heir, Czar Nicholas lived with his family in ease and luxury in magnificent palaces in Saint Petersburg and Moscow.

CATHERINE THE GREAT

Catherine II (1729–1796) was a German princess who married into the Russian royal family. Her husband (Peter the Great's grandson) became Czar Peter III in 1762, but he was disliked by powerful groups. Within months, he was murdered (probably with his wife's consent) and she had the Russian throne to herself. Catherine was a brilliant, highly educated woman, and a clever diplomat. She worked tirelessly to expand her realm west into Europe and east into Alaska. But she was ruthless to the poor peasants, making them little better than slaves.

Russia was the largest country in the world, sprawling from eastern Europe to the snowy forests of Siberia on the Pacific Ocean, and from the sunny warmth of the Black Sea in the south to the frozen Arctic Ocean. But the country had never caught up to Western Europe. Most people were still poor peasant farmers on Russia's vast plains. Until the mid-1800s, they had been half-enslaved, unable even to leave their lands without permission from their aristocratic landlords. Nicholas's grandfather, Alexander II, had made efforts to improve the peasants' lives. But he had been assassinated, and both his son and his grandson, Nicholas, had taken the side of the aristocrats. Was it time for the common people to overthrow the czar and his aristocrats, and create a workers' state of "comrades," in which everyone was equal? Talk of revolution had bubbled in the streets and workshops and universities of Moscow and Saint Petersburg for years, but the czar's secret police had rounded up most of the "troublemakers" and they had been shot or sent into exile in Siberia.

In 1917, the collapse of Russia's war-weary army brought down the rule of the Romanovs in a few weeks. Soldiers overthrew their officers. Aristocratic families fled or were slaughtered. Peasants took control of the land they had farmed for generations. In the cities, councils of workers overthrew the government and took power. Czar Nicholas gave up his throne, but he could not escape. The revolutionaries shot him and all his family.

After several years of civil war, Russia emerged as the Union of Soviet Socialist Republics, or Soviet Union. It became the first country in the world governed according to Communism, the theory advanced by the German thinker Karl Marx. "Soviets" were the councils of workers that had organized to lead the revolution. "Socialism" was the theory that, for the good of everyone, land and wealth and industry should be owned by the people as a whole, not by individuals. The flag showed a hammer and sickle, tools of the worker and farmer. But it was soon clear that, under Communism, power was held not by ordinary people – workers and farmers – but by the Communist Party, the tight-knit political organization that had taken charge of the revolution and created the new regime. The dictatorship of the Communist Party had replaced the dictatorship of the czars. The Communist Party planned the economy, deciding how best to build up industry and agriculture and to provide people with food and possessions.

Joseph Stalin, who fought his way to the top of the Communist Party, became more of a tyrant than any czar had been. During the 1930s, he and the Communist Party built up the armed forces of the Soviet Union and developed its industries and agriculture at any cost, seeking to make it a great power in the world. Stalin ruthlessly murdered his rivals in the Communist Party, and the party "liquidated" (got rid of) anyone who stood in its way. Millions of Russians were executed or shipped off to "gulags," labor camps in faraway Siberia, where most of them starved and died.

In 1932–33, as the Communist Party tried to change the way farming was done, the food crops failed almost completely. With their crops and animals gone, millions of farmers and their families starved to death, particularly in the Ukraine district. Few outside the region knew this was happening, for Stalin's government controlled all the newspapers. The Soviet Union had become a "totalitarian" society, one where the government totally controlled people's lives and resistance was not tolerated. Radios had only one station on the dial — the one that broadcast the government's version of events. Simply asking if things were going wrong could mean a one-way voyage to Siberia — or a bullet in the head.

The Rise of the Fuehrer

Russia was not the only country to find itself in the hands of a tyrant. After Germany was defeated in the Great War, Kaiser Wilhelm was forced to abdicate. Germany struggled through the 1920s, disorganized and impoverished, bitter about its loss and desperate to reclaim its place in the world. Its weak new democratic government was unable to solve these problems, and many Germans began falling under the spell of a new leader — not a Communist but a Nazi.

Picture this: it's September 1935, and the scene is the stadium in the German city of Nuremberg. In march thousands of men, in rigid formations, their boots crashing down in unison. They are troops from

the German army, members of the secret police, "Brownshirt" members of the Nazi Party, and young men from a group called Hitler Youth. They fill the Nuremberg stadium, surrounded by banners bearing the swastika, a Nazi symbol. Searchlights send pillars of light into the night sky as the men stand to be harangued by their leader, Adolf Hitler.

Two years earlier, Hitler had been elected chancellor of Germany. He and his Nazi party soon seized absolute power, promising to restore Germany's greatness, bring it back from its hardships, and punish the enemies of the German people. Many Germans responded positively to his message, and Hitler made himself the ruler, *der Fuehrer*, of Germany. At the Nuremberg Rally, he screamed out hatred and threats against foreigners and minorities, and the masses in the stadium chanted *"Heil Hitler"* in agreement.

Hitler brought more than threats and hatred. He focused the fears and resentments of Germany on Jewish people. To "purify" German blood, the Nazis banned marriages between Germans and Jews, and they stripped all the Jews in Germany of their citizenship. Three years later came Kristallnacht, a night of violent attacks against Jewish people and their businesses, homes, and synagogues. (The name celebrates the "crystals" of smashed glass.) Soon, people were being arrested, beaten, and sent to concentration camps just for being Jewish. Once again, Europe was in a turmoil of tension and hate.

The Great Depression

"Brother, can you spare a dime?" went a popular American song lyric in 1933. Even in the United States, the richest country in the world, millions of people were out of work – roaming the streets and looking for jobs, lining up at free "soup kitchens," and begging passersby for change. Men "rode the rails," jumping on railroad boxcars for a cheap ride to anywhere there might be work. Women scrimped and saved, making old clothes last another season, stretching a few vegetables into a meal for the children, worrying about the grocery bill and the rent. Times were bad, and no one knew when they would get better.

While Russia's Communist government insisted on controlling every aspect of the economy, Western countries believed in a "free market." Most businesses were privately run. They competed with each other, and the marketplace — the customers — decided what products were best, and what companies should be successful. But in 1929, something went wrong with the system.

It began on Wall Street, in New York City, the financial center of the United States. Business was booming, and prices on the stock market went higher – higher – too high. Then the bubble burst, the stock market collapsed, and the impact was felt all over the world. Companies in many countries had been barely staying in business since the Great War. Now that the banks were collapsing, company owners could not raise the money they needed to keep going. Workers lost their jobs. That meant they could not afford to buy things, and that put more people out of work, which meant they could not buy things either, and the circle went round and round. A quarter of all the workers in once-prosperous countries were unemployed. In the United States, most of the banks had closed down. Few people could afford to build new houses or buy new cars, or even to heat the houses and fuel the cars they had. Was this the collapse of the economic system that had kept Western countries prosperous for so long? Were democracy and the free market system a failure?

In Adolf Hitler's Germany, people were working at building weapons for the army, or on state projects like highways and dams. Stalin's Russia boasted of all the new steel mills and hydroelectric dams being built, all the tractors being delivered to collective (state-owned) farms, and there was no way for outsiders to judge the truth of the claims. Many people feared that the system of individual freedom, democratic governments, and economies that operated freely was doomed.

"The only thing we have to fear is fear itself," replied Franklin Roosevelt. Roosevelt was elected president of the United States in 1932, in the depths of the Great Depression, and he began changing the way the American economy was run. If banks could not lend and people could not spend, the government would do the spending needed to get people working again. The government hired hundreds of thousands of workers for conservation projects. It invested in highways and dams. It declared that people had to be protected against the inevitable ups and down of the marketplace. It began regulating businesses more closely, and it created "social security" programs: pensions for the elderly, welfare payments for the poor and unemployed. Roosevelt's plans reshaped the way governments worked and the way people lived throughout the free world.

But it wasn't Roosevelt who ended the Great Depression; it was something else. In 1939, just twenty-one years after the Great War that was supposed to put an end to war forever, the world plunged into another war.

World War Two

Blitzkrieg! The word means "lightning war" in German. When Adolf Hitler's armies tried to take over Europe, there was none of the deadly stalemate of trench warfare. His armies raced forward, led by tanks and motorized guns, with airplanes dive-bombing from above.

In the late 1930s, Hitler's Germany had started expanding. Desperate to avoid another war, Britain and France hoped the invasions would stop. But in 1939 Hitler invaded Poland. Britain and France, and Canada and almost all the other Commonwealth countries, declared war. Hitler's armies defeated Denmark and Norway and kept marching across Europe. France's defenses collapsed in a few days, and the Germans marched into Paris. In Western Europe, only Great Britain was left to stand against Hitler's might.

Next, Hitler invaded Russia and his armies drove deep into the land. But Stalin's dictatorship was stronger than the czar's regime had been. This time, Russia did not collapse.

World War Two swept across vast distances. It was fought in jungles and deserts and arctic wastes. Immense aircraft carriers maneuvered across the oceans, and submarines lurked beneath the waves. Heavy bombers flying in thousand-plane formations dumped explosives on sleeping cities. Million-man armies still marched and fought on foot, but this war ran on gasoline engines: armored tanks and guns to lead the attack, jeeps to carry messages behind the lines, and long lines of trucks bringing up supplies.

Once again, the United States hoped to stay out of the war. But Japan had entered the war as Germany's ally. On the morning of December 7, 1941, Japanese bombers, launched from aircraft carriers far away, swooped down without warning on peaceful Pearl Harbor in Hawaii. Much of the United States' Pacific fleet and air force sat there undefended, and in a few minutes most of the great battleships were exploding in flames and sinking at their moorings. Almost simultaneously, Japan struck at Hong Kong and the Philippines. Soon the Japanese army was overrunning much of East Asia and most of the islands of the western Pacific. The "Axis" powers – Germany, Japan, and Italy – had entered a global struggle against the "Allies" – the Soviet Union and the surviving democracies of the world, led by Prime Minister Winston Churchill of Britain and the American president, Franklin Roosevelt.

This was a larger war than the world had ever seen, fought with terrible brutality against soldiers and against civilians too. Gradually, the Allies overpowered the Axis armies and pushed the Japanese back toward their home islands. The Soviet armies stopped the Germans and began driving them back toward Germany. In June 1944, in the largest seaborne invasion ever seen, a vast fleet of ships delivered British, American, and Canadian soldiers onto the beaches of France. Slowly,

with terrible losses and destruction, the Allied powers overwhelmed the Axis. Adolf Hitler committed suicide as Russian armies marched into Berlin, the capital of Germany, at the end of April 1945. Three months later, Japan surrendered and World War Two was over. Fifty million people had died.

The Holocaust and the Bomb

The war was over, but the memories of two wartime nightmares are still haunting us. One was the atomic bomb. The other was the Holocaust.

In August 1945, the Allies had ended the war with Japan by dropping atomic bombs on the cities of Hiroshima and Nagasaki. Building these bombs had been an extraordinary effort of science and technology, carried on in great secrecy in the United States. The atomic bomb drew its power from the building blocks of the universe. By shattering atoms, a single bomb released more destructive force than any weapon before. It also unleashed massive, deadly radiation. The explosions obliterated Hiroshima and Nagasaki instantly. Tens of thousands of citizens were incinerated in a flash, and tens of thousands more died of burns and radiation poison in the days and years to come. Faced with total destruction, the Japanese Empire surrendered.

The atomic bombs saved the lives of many thousands of Allied soldiers and sailors, and citizens of the Allied countries cheered at the news of these super-weapons. But people soon realized that they could destroy the world. Before long, there were huge stockpiles of atomic weapons hundreds of times more powerful than those first bombs. War had been growing more terrible through the centuries. Now, it could destroy humanity itself.

The other nightmare of the war was genocide, the attempt to wipe out an entire people. Throughout the war, the Allies had been hearing grim rumors and bits of information about the Jews of Europe. The Nazis' hatred of Jewish people was well-known. Even before the war, Jews in Germany were being harassed, dismissed from their jobs, and generally persecuted. In the spring of 1945, as the Allies drove German troops out of the lands they had seized, they learned what else the Nazis had done. Throughout the areas they occupied during the war, the Nazis had rounded up Jewish people and shipped them to concentration camps. There, they had been worked to death, starved, or poisoned in gas chambers specially built to kill human beings by the thousand. They were not killed for their words or their actions, but simply for being who they were. About six million Jews had been murdered in these death factories, along with millions of Romanies ("Gypsies"), homosexuals, and other oppressed minorities, as well as the Nazis' political opponents. In Germany – one of the most prosperous and advanced nations in the world – the government had dedicated itself to systematically murdering innocent men, women, and children.

What could be done to avoid such horrors in the future? Around the world, an idea was brewing that nations could not remain above the law. Human beings had rights, and nations and peoples had to learn to settle their differences peaceably. In 1945, many countries came together to found the United Nations, a forum where they could meet together to try to prevent future wars. In 1948, the United Nations proclaimed the Universal Declaration of Human Rights. It said that everyone had the right to "life, liberty and security," to "equality before the law," to "freedom of movement" and "freedom of thought," and never to be tortured or held in slavery. Although many people were still denied these rights (and others set out in the Declaration), at least the world was saying out loud that these rights existed, for everyone, everywhere. Gradually these concepts became part of international law.

In 1946, in Nuremberg, the city where the Nazis had held their hate-filled rallies, the surviving leaders of Nazi Germany sat in a courtroom, being tried for crimes against humanity. For the first time ever, leaders who had started wars, murdered civilians, and tried to destroy whole populations were being held accountable before the law. They could now be tried, convicted, sentenced, and punished for their crimes against humanity.

GOLDA MEIR

Born in Ukraine and raised in the United States, Golda Meir (1898–1978) moved to Palestine in 1921. She was a leader of Zionism, the campaign to create an independent Israel. At first she worked in the labor movement, but after the founding of the state of Israel she held a series of political posts. In 1969 she became Israel's prime minister — the world's third female prime minister, after Sirimavo Bandaranaike of Sri Lanka, and Indira Gandhi of India. In 1973, when Arab countries suddenly attacked Israel on the Jewish holy day of Yom Kippur, she led her country through the war.

In 1948, part of Palestine, at the eastern end of the Mediterranean, became the state of Israel. Almost two thousand years after the destruction of their temple in Jerusalem, the Jewish people had a homeland of their own.

East against West

The end of World War Two did not put an end to tyranny. During the war, Stalin's Russian troops had conquered most of Eastern Europe. After it ended, the aging dictator turned many of those countries into "satellite" states, under Communist governments imposed by the Soviet Union. Germany itself was divided into two nations — West Germany, a democracy, and East Germany, a Communist dictatorship. Even Berlin, the capital city, was divided into West Berlin and East Berlin, and the Communist leaders built a wall through the city to keep their unhappy citizens from escaping to the other side. The "Berlin Wall" became a symbol of the hostility between West and East. Winston Churchill said that "an iron curtain has descended across the Continent."

What followed was a long, tense confrontation known as the "Cold War." It was "cold" because the nations were not actually fighting each other — but both sides bristled with hostility and suspicion. They spied on each other and kept vast armies facing each other in Central Europe. They built up immense supplies of nuclear weapons, and aircraft and missiles could deliver them to the enemy's homeland in minutes. Probably the only thing that kept the war "cold" was the knowledge that, no matter which side attacked first, a nuclear war would destroy them both.

For forty years the two "superpowers," the United States and the Soviet Union, competed to expand their influence around the globe. The United Nations was helpless to resolve the conflict. Any small crisis could bring the world to the edge of nuclear war.

But while the two sides were locked in confrontation, dramatic changes were happening in other parts of the world.

Turning Colonies into Nations

India had been on the front lines in World War Two. In a long, bitter campaign in the jungles and mountains of northeastern India and Burma, British forces had fought Japanese invaders who threatened the borders of India. Yet, at the same time, Gandhi and the political party called the Indian National Congress continued to insist that India could rule itself, and that the British had no right to control the lives of millions of Indians. When the war ended, Britain was weakened and exhausted and could no longer resist these demands for freedom. After almost half a century of preaching his message of *satyagraha*, peaceful resistance, Gandhi saw his prediction – that the cause of freedom could triumph without violence – beginning to come true. The peaceful strikes, marches, and boycott campaigns he had promoted had made Britain's colonial rule impossible.

INDIRA GANDHI

Indira Gandhi (1917–1984) was not related to Mahatma Gandhi, but worked as an assistant to her father, Jawaharlal Nehru, India's first prime minister. She was a government minister for the next prime minister, and became prime minister herself in 1966. She was a strong and determined leader in both peacetime and wartime, and tried hard to eliminate hunger in India. But she grew dictatorial and intolerant, persecuting those who criticized her, and she lost the 1977 election. In 1980 she regained the leadership but in 1984, after violent conflict with Indians of the Sikh religion, she was murdered by her Sikh bodyguards.

At midnight on August 15, 1947, India became the first large non-European colony of Britain to achieve independence. Much to Gandhi's regret, however, it did not become independent as a single country. It was partitioned into Pakistan, which was mostly Muslim, and India, which was mostly Hindu. Gandhi had always insisted that different peoples must learn to live together, respecting each other's differences, but not everyone believed that was possible. Hatreds and tensions continued. Hindus and Muslims killed each other by the millions at the time of independence. Six months after independence, Gandhi himself was shot dead — by an assassin who was, like Gandhi, a Hindu.

Like Britain, the rest of Europe could no longer rule so many foreign territories against the will of the people who lived there. The European powers had lost the wealth, military power, and moral authority to dominate others the way they had for three hundred years. A great wave of "decolonization" began. In just a few years, from the mid-1950s to the mid-1960s, nearly all the European colonies in Africa became independent states. The same thing happened across the Middle East, and throughout Southeast Asia, and in the island states of the Caribbean and the South Pacific. Some countries went to war to win their independence. More often, though, they gained their freedom peacefully. In a very short time, dozens of new countries were added to the map. They became member states of the United Nations, unfurled new flags, and sang new national anthems.

Independence did not make life easy in the new states. Many of the nations had been left very poor, and they had few citizens trained or prepared to run governments or build up the societies now left in their hands. Some were torn apart by tribal rivalries and struggles for power. Many began as democracies but quickly fell into the hands of dictators and military strongmen. Many became poorer, more violent, and more corrupt than they had been as colonies, and it would take decades for them to rebuild themselves. Still, the world had changed remarkably. When leaders gathered at the United Nations, or when athletes gathered at the Olympic Games, they were no longer mostly white men of European origin. The world was now represented by men and women of every skin color, every kind of national dress. Although the first leaders of the United Nations were

European men, in 1961 U Thant, from the newly independent South Asian state of Burma, became secretary-general. Since then, some of his successors have come from Peru, Egypt, Ghana, and South Korea. The leadership of the world was finally beginning to resemble the people of the world. As once-colonized nations began asserting their equality, other oppressed groups began asserting theirs as well.

Black and White

On December 1, 1955, in Montgomery, Alabama, in the United States, Rosa Parks refused to give up her seat on a city bus to a white man. Even though the Civil War had ended slavery in America a century before, prejudice against black people remained strong. Blacks were prevented from voting, they could not get an education equal to that of whites, and most jobs were closed to them. They could not share restaurants, trains, or bus

ROSA PARKS   NELSON MANDELA

seats reserved for white people. Now they were taking a stand against this oppression. After Parks was removed from the bus and arrested, the black community of Montgomery refused to ride the city's buses at all. A young minister, Martin Luther King Jr., became a leader in the "bus boycott." Across the American south, descendants of slaves began to demand the rights that all American citizens deserved.

Less than eight years later, Martin Luther King spoke to a quarter of a million people from the steps of the Abraham Lincoln Memorial in Washington, D.C. Since the Rosa Parks bus boycott, King had become the leader of a mass movement to ensure the civil rights of black Americans. King had learned from Mahatma Gandhi. He too believed that nonviolent resistance would lead to peaceful change, though his home was firebombed and many of his supporters suffered arrests, beatings, threats, and even death. "I have a dream," he told the crowds in Washington, "that one day this nation will rise up and live out the true meaning of its creed . . . that all men are created equal." A year later, the United States passed a Civil Rights Act that put an end to the racist laws that men and women like Rosa Parks had endured for a century, and the campaign for equality moved forward. Four years after that, King was dead, shot down by an assassin.

The Rosa Parks bus boycott inspired protesters as far away as South Africa. Black people were the majority there, but the country was tightly controlled by a white population that had settled there many generations earlier. The government of South Africa had developed a system called "apartheid," which officially meant "separate development," but really meant that blacks faced cruel discrimination in their own land.

Although Gandhi had first formed his ideas about passive resistance in South Africa, the African National Congress, the leader in the struggle against oppression, despaired of nonviolent resistance and decided to use bombings and sabotage and other violent means. Soon, most of its leaders were either exiled or jailed as terrorists. Nelson Mandela, the leader of the Congress, spent twenty-seven years in a South African jail. During his long imprisonment, he pondered the need for reconciliation in his country. Meanwhile, worldwide support for the campaign against apartheid grew stronger. In 1990, Mandela was released from prison to begin negotiations with the South African government. In 1994, apartheid was peacefully overthrown. In the first free elections in South Africa, Mandela was elected president. By the time he retired in 1999, he had become a worldwide symbol of peace and equality and reconciliation. Martin Luther King's dream – Gandhi's dream – seemed closer to becoming reality.

Good Rocking Tonight

The young truck driver came into Sun Records in Memphis, Tennessee, in 1954, hoping to record some songs. The producer did not like any of them very much. They took a break and the truck driver, Elvis Presley, began fooling around with a tune recorded years before by a black artist named Arthur Crudup. Back in 1954, white singers like Elvis were not supposed to combine black "rhythm and blues" with the "country" music that white southerners sang. But Elvis tried it out. "That's it!" said the producer. The song "That's All Right Now, Mama" was the sound he was looking for.

Soon, Elvis was the hottest singing star in the world. Rock 'n' roll was here to stay.

There was a boom going on — a baby boom. All through the Depression and World War Two, people had hardly dared to start families. When the war was over, they made up for lost time. Before long, there were more kids around than there had been for generations. It was a time of prosperity and optimism. People had automobiles, and portable radios to play the new music at home or away. They went to drive-in movies, and some could watch flickering black-and-white pictures on their own television sets. Kids no longer had to go to work when they were twelve or fifteen to help support their families. They stayed in school longer, and they had more pocket money to spend. They wanted their own music — rock 'n' roll. It helped that you could dance to it. It helped that it was simple to play, so it was easy to get a band together. It even helped that older people hated it.

RADIO AND TELEVISION

In 1901, the Italian scientist Guglielmo Marconi sent the letter S, in Morse Code, across the Atlantic Ocean — not by transatlantic telegraph cable but through the air, on radio waves. Before long, speech and music could be transmitted without wires. By the 1920s, families gathered around large home radios and listened to news and songs and church sermons. Along came television, delivering home entertainment with black-and-white pictures; then color television; then satellite television, beaming TV programs around the globe from orbiting hardware; then flat-screen TVs, cellphone TVs, in-car TVs, security TVs — inescapable TV.

As the "baby boomers" grew up, young people continued to develop their own style. In the 1960s a band from England called the Beatles became a sensation, though at first they were as famous for their pudding-bowl haircuts as for their inventive music. Soon afterwards, a new movement began in California and spread around the world. The "hippies" rejected conformity and order and promoted peace and love and psychedelic drugs. Ideas of change, of rebellion against convention, were in the air. Many young people were opposed to a war that the United States was fighting in South Vietnam, a small country in Southeast Asia, and this increased their determination to resist the established order of society.

Women took up the cause of change as well. In Western countries, there had been a great wave of campaigning for women's rights in Queen Victoria's day. Around the time of the Great War, women had acquired the right to vote in most Western countries, but most kinds of paid work were still done by men, while housework and childcare were considered "women's work." During the 1960s, women began asserting their right to work in the same jobs as men, to receive equal pay for equal work, and to share equally in public activities and family decision-making. The feminist movement insisted on doing away with traditional notions that women were weak, vulnerable creatures who needed to be controlled and protected by men.

The End of the Cold War

On November 9, 1989, crowds surged from East Berlin into West Berlin. They climbed the wall that divided the city, and used sledgehammers to smash it to pieces. They danced and cheered and scooped up chunks of concrete for souvenirs. It was a historic moment. Berlin was one city again. The Iron Curtain had fallen.

This was not the first rejection of the Communist system. Citizens had risen in rebellion in Hungary in the 1950s, in Czechoslovakia in the 1960s, and in Poland in the 1970s. In the end, though, change came not from the satellite states but in the Soviet Union itself. In the 1980s a new leader, Mikhail Gorbachev, called for an era of "glasnost" (openness) and "perestroika" (restructuring) in the way the Soviet Union worked. Premier Gorbachev hoped that such changes, carefully controlled, would allow the Communist system to continue. But the small reforms he permitted let in a flood of change, for the system had become too ineffective and too corrupt to survive. The Soviet Union began to collapse. Its satellite states quickly regained their independence and became democratic nations of Europe once again. Germany was reunited, and by 1991 the Soviet Union itself had vanished. Ukraine and small Baltic states that had long been controlled by Russia became independent again. Russia was reborn as a smaller, weaker state, a vulnerable democracy, no longer such a threat to the rest of the world. The Cold War was over.

But Communism was not yet finished. In China, after decades of civil war, foreign interference, and Japanese occupation, the Communist Party of Mao Zedong had defeated its rivals. In 1949 Mao established the People's Republic of China. Like Stalin, Mao was determined to modernize his country at any cost. Under his brutal, authoritarian dictatorship, China was isolated from the rest of the world. The state planned everything and controlled everything. Millions died in famines, millions more in radical campaigns to restructure Chinese society. Dissent was ruthlessly crushed. But China remained poor and backward.

Deng Xiaoping had been a loyal follower of Mao Zedong throughout the Chinese Revolution, but he had been "purged" in one of the many power struggles that rocked the Communist Party; he was lucky not to be shot. Slowly, Deng worked his way back into the inner circles of power, and in the 1980s he introduced a startling new idea. He admitted that the Communist program of central planning had not succeeded in building a strong economy, and he proposed "socialism with Chinese characteristics" – a system in which the Communist Party would retain absolute power, but private business would be unleashed to help develop the economy. His suggestion would change China dramatically.

Freed from the Communist Party's central planning, China surged forward. It was, after all, the largest country in the world, and it had endless resources and millions of people. In the 1990s it grew more rapidly than almost any other country. Sleepy villages transformed themselves into industrial cities producing high-technology goods for global export. Poor farmers trudging behind their oxen in the rice paddies turned into business people, and some became fabulously rich. Suddenly China was the greatest success story in world business, and the source of a large part of the world's products. The Industrial Revolution had finally come to the oldest civilization in the world.

In the summer of 2008, China showed off its new wealth and confidence when it welcomed the world to a spectacular Olympic Games in the capital city, Beijing. Chinese athletes won more medals than competitors from any other country. China's long humiliation seemed over, with a new future awaiting the nation as its people became prosperous and educated and sought the freedom to choose their own lives and careers.

Saving the Planet

"I would like to say something about this land. The only food I like is meat." The speaker was an Inuit (Eskimo) elder from the Arctic islands in the far north of Canada. He was trying to explain how the world seemed to his people, one of the last hunting and gathering peoples on the planet. He had grown up among people who lived on the land in one of the harshest places on earth. They had been just a few families following the seals and musk ox and other animals across the expanses of land and frozen sea. They wore clothes made of skins. They ate raw meat. They knew how to make snow houses, knew when the seals they hunted would come to the hole in the ice to breathe, knew how to fight a polar bear if they had to.

Now it was the twenty-first century, and the world had become very crowded for hunting and gathering peoples. In some remote places – the deserts of the Kalahari, in Africa, or the jungles of the Amazon, in

South America – a few traditional societies lived on, but here in the Arctic, the traditional way of life was disappearing. People had moved into villages and grown used to medical care and schooling, and packaged food from the south, and television. Their lives were better and safer. If, one season, the seals did not come to the air hole, families did not starve to death as they once had. But the elder knew that his people had given something up. There seemed to be no room on the planet for people to live the life of his ancestors. There were fewer birds in the sky, fewer whales in the water. Fishing fleets took most of the fish. It seemed to him that, after so many thousands of years, the hunter-gatherers were at the verge of extinction. And perhaps they were not the only ones at risk.

Back when everyone was a hunter-gatherer, the small human population lived lightly upon the earth. With agriculture and a growing population, the impact of humans became greater. Fertile valleys turned into deserts, and lush green forests were cut down, leaving rocky hillsides where the soil washed away and nothing grew. Wild animals were driven out and replaced by cattle and sheep.

Industrial civilization was an even greater burden on the planet. The population had grown to about a billion people by the year 1900. By 2000 it was more than six billion. Humanity was taking over all the wild lands of the world, and endangering many of the wild animals. Would whales survive in the oceans? Would tigers be able to exist in Asia's dwindling patches of jungle? Would the elephants and mountain gorillas of East Africa be hunted to extinction? If the mountains of Mexico were logged, would the monarch butterflies ever return there on their long migration from up north? At the end of the twentieth century, the largest mass extinction in tens of millions of years was taking place, and the main cause was simple: too many human beings.

When the fishers of England and France and Spain first came to Newfoundland around 1500 CE, they said the supply of codfish was so vast that it would be impossible for them to even start reducing it. For five hundred years the local fishers and the fleets of a hundred fishing nations came to the Newfoundland area to draw from those endless stocks. Until 1999, when suddenly there were no more cod. Scientists struggled to explain this. They spoke of shifting ocean currents, and changes in water temperatures, and a thousand other things science barely understood. But one fisherman thought he knew the most important cause. Let's face it, he said, "We have caught them all."

In the sunbaked deserts of Saudi Arabia, the country with the largest known reserves of oil on the planet, oil wells pump around the clock. Elsewhere in the world, wells pump oil from deep below the Arctic waters of northern Alaska, from beneath the warm, shallow waters of the Gulf of Mexico and the stormy waters off Scotland and Norway and Newfoundland. Oil flows from Nigeria in West Africa, from under the forests of Alberta in Canada and the steppes of Russia and the jungles of Venezuela in South America. Huge pipelines cross the continents, and some of the largest ships ever built carry oil across the sea to supply thirsty consumers all over the world.

The twentieth century was oil's century. Ever since Manchester began burning coal to drive its textile factories in the 1700s, we have been learning to expand our power by burning fuels. After the first oil wells were drilled in North America in the 1850s, oil became the fuel of prosperity and power. New products to make our lives easier, all kinds of new vehicles to get us quickly wherever we wanted to go, sprawling cities and factories – they all ran on oil, oil, oil.

Now we have pumped up and burned away millions of years of oil production, and we are unlikely to find more cheap, easy sources. What will we use to fuel our societies and our lives?

There is another problem. Human civilization blossomed at the end of an ice age. As the earth became much warmer ten thousand years ago, we seized the opportunity to populate the world and to learn to farm it. Now, however, the energy we have burned, the oil we have turned into heat, is escaping into the sky, warming the earth even more. Is it possible that human beings are causing another major shift in global temperature, as great as the one that transformed our life ten thousand years ago? And if we are, what will become of our civilizations?

A View from Afar

In 1968, the first humans ever to leave our planet broke out of their orbit around earth and headed to the moon, in a space capsule that would carry them behind it, past its mysterious "dark side," and back home. Because that test run went so well, more astronauts headed into space in July 1969. One of them, a quiet American named Neil Armstrong, became the first human being to walk on the moon. "That's one small step for a man, one giant leap for mankind," he said, as his boot left the spacecraft and came down on the dusty surface of the moon.

Something just as important had happened on that earlier mission, the one that returned home without landing on the moon. From their orbiting ship, the three astronauts had been the first people to see the earth as a small globe floating in the empty blackness of space.

Their photographs gave the world a new image of our planet: a pale blue dot, a wondrous and fragile place in a cold and inhospitable universe.

The moon landings showed some of the best qualities of the human species. The very first human to travel into space was Yuri Gagarin of the Soviet Union, who orbited the earth in 1961. Just eight years later, brilliant science, brilliant

THE INTERNET

In the 1960s, in the height of the Cold War, the United States military invented the Internet as a way to maintain communications if there was another world war. In the 1970s, some universities and some other countries began to link up with the system. By the 1980s, companies were developing networks to connect their divisions; eventually, they joined up with the Internet. As more and more systems became part of the Net, more and more of the world could communicate instantly, by electronic mail. In 1991, with the establishment of the World Wide Web, pictures and sound could be sent as well as words. So many brilliant inventions of the past — paper and printing, telegraph, telephone, radio, TV — are being duplicated by this powerful Space Age network.

engineering, an enormous effort of teamwork and construction, and a great deal of skill and bravery had taken astronauts to the moon and back.

Today, there is an International Space Station in permanent orbit above the earth. Most of our television programs and many of our telephone calls come to us by way of space satellites. People from many lands have traveled into space. In prosperous countries, nearly every household has a computer much more powerful than the ones that guided the astronauts to the moon and back.

Human beings are an amazingly inventive species — always exploring, always experimenting. Today we have more knowledge and more opportunities for new discoveries than ever before. If we can keep in mind the image of that small blue dot in the darkness of space, the rich and beautiful planet we are so lucky to be born on, perhaps we can use our ingenuity to protect ourselves and our precious home planet from the dangers that we ourselves have created.

The GLOBAL CITY

When I was starting this book, I walked out into the city where my family and I live. Our city could be Hamburg in Germany, Rio de Janeiro in Brazil, the Asian city-state of Singapore, Miami in the United States of America, Lagos or Cape Town in Africa, or Melbourne in Australia. It happens that the city where we live is Toronto, in southern Canada, on the shore of one of the Great Lakes of North America.

Another day in the global city: Japanese cars, South Asian headgear, European sports, Jamaican music, Brazilian coffee, American styles. People? From everywhere.

HAGGIS

Even plain old meat and veggies can be turned into unusual food – like haggis, Scotland's national dish. There are many recipes for haggis, but most go something like this. *Mix oatmeal and onions with spices and fat and meat stock. Cook the chopped-up heart, liver, and lungs of a sheep and add them to the oatmeal. Stuff this mixture into a sheep's stomach (without the rest of the sheep) and boil for three hours. Be sure to prick a few holes in the stomach so it doesn't explode.* According to the Scottish poet Robbie Burns, the result is the "great chieftain" of puddings.

People I meet in the subway cars, streets, and workplaces of Toronto are a varied group. They do not all look the same, or speak the same languages, or look back to the same countries as their homelands. Some Torontonians are of the Anishnabe or the Seneca Nation. They have been here forever, you might say, descendants of aboriginal nations that have lived here since the ancient glaciers melted. Not far from my house is a place where a Seneca town once stood above the river that leads inland from the lake. The very name "Toronto" comes from a Seneca word.

My country, Canada, is a child of world history, once a colony of France, then taken over by Great Britain in one of the wars those European nations fought. When the city of Toronto began to grow, its people were mostly English, Scottish, and Irish, some coming directly from Britain, others moving from the new United States of America. There was a Jewish neighborhood by the early 1900s, and a French-Canadian neighborhood, and migrants from other European nations, and a few Chinese who first came to Canada to build its railroads. But until recently, Toronto remained a very British city.

Later in the twentieth century, Canada opened its doors to the world. That was world history too. When my family came to Canada, leaving behind the hardships Britain had suffered in the years after World War Two, we were some of the last specially privileged British migrants. Soon after, new ideas about human rights transformed Canada's immigration policies. There's now a Toronto neighborhood where a quarter of a million people hit the streets when Italy wins the World Cup of soccer, and another neighborhood with nearly as many people celebrating in Portuguese when the Brazilians win. In Little India, you find twenty kinds of mangoes, brilliantly colored fabrics, blazing hot spices, and Bollywood movies. There are Chinese neighborhoods where people do business in several Chinese languages. Japanese, Koreans, and people from the Philippines are well represented too.

South Asians live in Toronto, as well. Sikhs, Muslims, and Hindus have all immigrated here. There are former Christian churches that have become mosques or temples or *gurdwaras* as new faith communities have taken their place alongside older ones. Sometimes I hear Spanish speakers on the street or in the subway. These might be migrants from the Philippines or people who have come to Canada by way of Mexico or Chile, heirs of the long Spanish presence in South and Central America.

Toronto moves to reggae and afrobeat, too, for people here have roots in Africa. Some of Toronto's African-Canadian citizens are descended from men and women who "followed the North Star" to a place where slavery had been abolished. Some have come recently from Somalia, Ghana, Morocco, and other African nations. Many have come from Jamaica or Barbados, where their ancestors were brought unwillingly from Africa hundreds of years ago. Because Trinidad had its own migration from India, Toronto's Trinidadians have Asian as well as African roots.

Toronto declares that it is the most multicultural city in the world. Perhaps it is. But it is not so different from Manchester or Rio or Melbourne.

Migrations are transforming cities all over the world. Countries look for skilled immigrants, and people in many regions are eager to escape from hardship or to build better lives. Airlines carry people around the globe in a few hours, and millions of us fly between the continents every year. People come to Toronto, and Torontonians go to live and work on other continents. The next new celebrities, discoveries, or political challenges may come from anywhere. Huge inequalities still exist on the planet, but we are a moving, mixing world.

There are people from every continent on every other continent now, and our human species is mixing back together. In our global cities, Latinos become neighbors with Africans. Asians marry Europeans. Europeans embrace Buddhism and Islam, and Koreans or Kenyans may be devout Christians. People proclaim their Jewish-Ukrainian-Scottish-Cantonese-Cherokee roots. Fifty or a hundred years ago, some people imagined they could subdivide the people of the world into distinct and separate races. Today, more and more people have some genes from Europe, some from Asia, some from North America.

This is a new moment in our history. We were all one people fifty thousand years ago. Then our human species spread around the globe. We settled separate continents and grew apart for tens of thousands of years. Small changes and adaptations in our genes produced the pale northern peoples, the dark-haired Asians, the dark-skinned Africans and Australians, and everyone else too. Ways to be human became gloriously different all over the world.

Now the world is bringing all those different ways together again.

INDEX

A

Africa, 5-6, 7, 10, 11, 13, 15, 23, 29, 31, 33, 49-50, 59, 80, 88, 90, 99, 101, 103, 104, 105, 106, 126, 128, 134, 135, 136, 139, 155, 168, 176, 177; and San bushmen, 31

Alexander II, Czar (Russia), 156

Alexander the Great, 69

Americas, 5, 7, 11, 12-13, 15, 28-29, 31, 33, 46, 91; Central America, 23, 35, 46, 75, 86, 99, 105; North America, 7, 28, 31, 49, 89, 90, 100-102, 105, 139, 177; South America, 7-8, 9, 19, 29, 49, 75, 90, 98, 99, 100, 112, 126, 141, 177

Animals: domestication of, 21, 22, 24, 29-31, 84, 101, 176; and extinction of species, 11-13, 26, 131, 176; in the Ice Age, 12-13, 26; introduction of to the New World, 101-102; represented in cave paintings, 10-11, 15; symbolic importance of, 15, 16, 39, 44, 55

Armstrong, Neil, 178

Asia, 5, 7, 10, 12, 15, 83, 105, 141, 176; Central Asia, 6, 29, 30, 64, 101, 102; Southeast Asia, 6, 8, 11, 56, 59, 88, 95, 96, 99, 101, 168

Atahualpa, Emperor (Incas), 99, 100

Attila the Hun, 75, 79

Augustus, Caesar, 73

Australia, 5, 6, 9, 10, 11, 12-13, 19, 22, 31, 60, 90, 96, 99-100, 101, 147; Aborigines of, 22, 31, 60

Austria, 107, 112, 147; Austria-Hungary, 148

Aztec Empire, 28, 97-98; and city of Tenochtitlán, 97-98

B

Belgium, 113, 135

Bell, Alexander Graham, 123

Bolívar, Simón, 112

Bonaparte, Napoleon, 111-13, 134, 147

Brazil, 31, 99, 103, 104, 183

Britain, 11, 70, 71, 78, 83, 89, 113, 134-35, 148, 149, 150, 152, 161, 162, 182-83; British Empire, 99, 117, 134-35, 136-37, 138, 141, 146, 147, 153, 154, 167; industrialization in, 115, 115-18, 128, 134, 177

C

Cabot, John, 95

Caesar, Julius, 71-72

Cambodia, 51, 131; and Angkor Wat, 51

Canada, 100, 127, 128, 139, 141, 146, 147, 150, 161, 162, 177, 181-84; immigration to, 182-84; Newfoundland and Labrador, 18, 90, 95, 103, 176-77; settlement at L'Anse aux Meadows, 90

Capitalism (free market), 130, 160

Caribbean Islands, 103, 104, 105, 112, 146, 168

Carnegie, Andrew, 121

Catherine II (the Great) (Russia), 155, 156

Champlain, Samuel de, 100-101

Charlemagne, 77, 77-78, 85, 89

Charles I, King (England), 108

Charles II, King (England), 108

China, 6, 8, 21, 23, 25-27, 29, 35-39, 42, 46, 50, 56, 57, 59, 60, 83, 85-89, 95, 96, 119-20, 126, 138-39, 140, 174; Communism in, 174-75; emigration from, 138-39, 182; and exploration, 88-89, 91; Great Wall of, 37; industrialization in, 140, 175; and the Terracotta Army, 38-39

Christianity, 53, 58-59, 60, 74, 77, 79, 80, 98, 135, 139, 140, 141; and the Crusades, 81-82, 85, 107; and missionaries, 79, 98, 135, 138, 140; persecution of by Roman Empire, 59, 73; the Protestant Church, 105-107; Quakers, 141

Churchill, Winston, 162, 166

Cixi, Empress Dowager (China), 138

Cleopatra, 72

Cold War, 166, 173

Colonization, 95, 98, 99-100, 103, 104-105, 108-109, 117, 135, 140, 146, 147, 151, 155; and colonial independence, 167-69

Columbus, Christopher, 93, 93-95, 96, 101, 103, 105, 151

Communism, 157, 160, 166, 173 75

Constantine, Emperor (Rome), 74, 80

Copernicus, 120

Cortés, Hernán, 96-98, 112, 135

Crazy Horse, 146

Crops: coffee, 102, 103, 104; corn (maize), 21, 23, 28, 46, 49, 100; cotton, 103, 104, 142; rice (oryza), 21, 25-27, 49, 85-86, 102, 120, 138; sugar cane, 102, 103, 104, 138-39; Three Sisters (corn, beans, and squash), 28, 102; tobacco, 29, 103, 104, 142; wheat, 23-24, 26, 102; wild vs. domesticated, 23-24

Crusades, 81-82, 85, 107

Custer, George, 146

Cyrus, King (Persia), 63-65, 68, 85

Czechoslovakia, 173

D

da Vinci, Leonardo, 85

Dalai Lama, 56

Darius, King (Persia), 66

Darwin, Charles, 120

Deng Xiaoping, 174

Depression, 159-61, 172

Disease, spread of, 32, 42, 83-84, 96, 100-102, 103, 150; Black Death, 83-84, 101

E

Earth: age of, 4; and climate change, 6, 11-13, 22, 177-78; effects of industrialization on, 176-78; and Ice Age, 5-7, 9, 14, 26, 177

Ecuador, 49, 98

Edward VII, King (Britain), 147

Egypt, 30, 40, 42, 43-46, 53, 58, 64, 69, 71, 72, 169; the Great Pyramid of Giza, 43; religious beliefs in, 44, 58; Valley of the Kings, 43, 45-46

Egyptian pharaohs: Hatshepsut, 43-46, 45, 53; Khufu (Cheops), 43; Ramses the Great, 46;

Thutmose, 44; Thutmose III, 46; Tutankhamen, 46

Elizabeth I, Queen (England), 105-106, 107

Empires, 35-51, 64; African (Mwene Mutapa), 49-51; Assyrian, 63, 63-68; Babylonian, 53-54, 61, 63; Byzantine, 74, 80; Chinese (Shi Huangdi), 35-39, 42; Egyptian (Hatshepsut), 43-46; Khmer (Cambodia), 51; Mogul, 136-37; Ottoman, 80; Persian, 69, 70; Sumerian, 39-43, 41; *see also entries for* Aztec Empire; Britain: British Empire; Incan Empire; Mayan Empire; Roman Empire

England, 81, 84, 85, 105-109, 115, 117, 118, 128, 133, 154, 176, 182; emigration from, 182; industrialization in, 115-18, 128, 177; *see also* Britain

Ericson, Leif, 89

Europe, 5, 6, 7, 9, 10, 11, 12, 15, 30, 31, 33, 64, 77-85, 119, 126; Black Death in, 83-84; Dark Ages in, 75; emigration from, 147, 182; exploration and colonies of, 89-91, 93-105, 120, 135, 138-39, 146, 147, 151, 155; industrialization in, 120-21, 138, 147; Napoleonic Wars in, 111-13, 148-49; racism in, 141; Renaissance in, 85

Exploration, 89-91, 93, 93-105; of the Americas, 95, 96-102

F

Farmers, 3, 16, 19, 24, 31, 39, 45, 46-47, 49, 54, 60, 80, 82, 83, 84, 100, 115-16, 118-19, 126-29, 131, 138, 156, 157-58, 177; advantages and disadvantages faced by, 25, 32-33, 41-42; sacred beliefs of, 54, 60

Feminist movement, 173

Feudalism, 79-80, 128-29

Ford, Henry, 122, 123-25, 129

France, 10, 11, 78, 81, 83, 85, 89, 100, 105, 107, 108, 109, 110-13, 136, 147, 148, 149, 150, 161, 162, 176, 182; and French Revolution, 110-11

Franks, 78, 79

G

Gagarin, Yuri, 178

Galileo, 120

Gandhi, Indira, 165, 167

Gandhi, Mohandas (Mahatma), 153-55, 167-68, 170, 171; and "peaceful resistance," 154, 155, 167

Genghis Khan, 30

Germany, 73, 78, 81, 83, 107-108, 112, 121, 133, 135, 138, 146-47, 148, 150, 151, 157, 158-59, 160, 162, 163, 164, 165; division and reunification of, 166, 173, 174; industrialization in, 121

Gorbachev, Mikhail, 173-74

Greece, ancient, 57-58, 60, 63, 65-69, 71, 80, 85, 88, 119, 134; arts and culture in, 65, 68-69, 71, 85; and "democracy," 66, 69, 80, 108, 130; sacred beliefs of, 57-58, 60, 68

Greenland, 7, 89

H

Hammurabi, 53, 53-54, 61; code of, 53-54, 61

Herders, 29-31, 39, 49, 50

Herodotus, 69

Hinduism, 53, 55, 56, 57, 60, 136, 154, 155, 168, 183

"Hippie" movement, 172-73

Hitler, Adolf, 159, 160, 161-63

Holland, 82, 84, 99, 105, 107, 108-109, 155; exploration and colonies of, 84-85, 99, 100, 108

Holocaust, 163, 164-65

Homo sapiens, 4, 5; migration and adaptation of, 5-9, 11-16, 90; *see also* Hunter-gatherers; Farmers; Herders

Hungary, 173

Hunter-gatherers, 3, 3-19, 21-33, 50, 119, 131, 175, 177; migration of, 14-16, 22; sacred beliefs of, 9-11, 15, 16-17, 18, 54

I

Ice Age, 5-7, 9, 14, 26, 177; and climate change, 11-13, 22, 177

Iceland, 83, 89

Incan Empire, 28, 97, 98-99, 100; and Machu Picchu, 99

India, 6, 25, 26, 41, 43, 50, 55-56, 59, 60, 64, 69, 80, 83, 88, 95, 99, 103, 112, 117, 126, 128, 153, 154-55, 165, 167-68; emigration from, 138 39; as part of British Empire, 134, 136-37, 154; and self-rule, 167-68; and the Taj Mahal, 136, 137

Industrialization, 115, 115-31, 140, 176; coal as fuel for, 116, 117, 121, 177; and mass production, 120, 124, 125, 129; and move to cities, 126, 128; oil and gas as fuel for, 123, 125, 127, 177; working conditions created by, 118, 121, 130

Inventions, 88, 119, 120-21: aircraft, 150; automobiles, 122, 123-25; calendars, 41, 47, 72; diesel engine, 121; electrical power, 123, 127; gunpowder, 87, 88, 119; Internet, 179; papermaking and printing, 30, 86-87, 88; radio and television, 172; steam power, 116, 117, 121, 122, 127; telegraph, 122; telephone, 122, 123; writing, 40-41, 47

Ireland, 89, 106, 182

Isabella I, Queen (Spain), 94

Islam, 59, 60, 75, 80-82, 94, 106, 107, 119, 136, 167-68, 183

Israel, 58, 165, 166; and Zionism, 165

Italy, 60, 66, 70, 71, 75, 78, 83, 107, 112, 135, 146-47, 162

J

Japan, 56, 139-41, 147, 162, 163, 167, 174; and bombing of Hiroshima, Nagasaki, 163, 164

Jerusalem, 58, 60, 81, 82

Judaism, 58-59, 60, 166; persecution of Jews by Nazis, 159, 163, 164-65

K

King, Martin Luther, Jr., 170, 171

Kublai Khan, 30, 86

L

Lee, Robert E., 143-45

Lincoln, Abraham, 143, 145

Livingstone, David, 135, 141

Louis XVI, King (France), 111

Luther, Martin, 106

M

Magellan, Ferdinand, 95-96

Mandela, Nelson, 169, 170-71

Mao Zedong, 174

Maori civilization, 9

Marconi, Guglielmo, 172

Mark Antony, 72

Marx, Karl, 130, 157

Mayan Empire, 28, 35, 46-49, 50-51, 64, 86; accomplishments of, 47; and Chichén Itzá, 48; ritual ball game of, 35, 48, 51; sacred beliefs of, 35, 48-49

M'Bandi, Nzinga, Queen (Africa), 136

Meiji Emperor (Japan), 140, 147

Meir, Golda, 165

Mesopotamia, 40, 50, 53, 59, 63

Mexico, 21, 28, 35, 46, 47, 48, 86, 96-98, 99, 105, 176

Middle East, 5, 6, 26, 29, 30, 40, 46, 57, 59, 60, 63, 71, 75, 81, 86, 88, 106, 119, 168

Mongols, 30, 86, 101

Montezuma, Emperor (Aztec), 97

Morse, Samuel, 122; and Morse Code, 122

N

Nabateans, 66

Napoleon III, Emperor (France), 147

Natives (North America), 8, 18, 60, 99, 145-46; Anasazi, 102; Anishnabe, 182; and Battle of Little Bighorn, 146; Blackfoot, 101, 134; Cheyenne, 31, 101, 146; Inuit, 31, 175; Longhouse people, 28; Mi'kmaq, 100-101; "Mound Builders," 28, 100; Plains Cree, 31; Seneca, 182; Sioux, 31, 101, 146

Nazi Party, 158-59, 164, 165

New Guinea, 6, 19, 23

New Zealand, 9, 99-100

Nicholas II, Czar (Russia), 155-57

Norway, 31, 83, 133, 161, 177; Sami people of, 31

P

Pakistan, 167

Palestine, 70, 78, 165, 166

Parks, Rosa, 169, 169-70

Persia, 63, 63-68, 69, 70, 85

Peru, 28, 49, 98, 105, 169; and Machu Picchu, 99

Peter III, Czar (Russia), 156

Peter the Great (Russia), 155

Philip II, King (Spain), 105, 107

Philippines, 96, 100, 146, 162

Pizarro, Francisco, 98-99, 112, 135

Poland, 84, 161, 173

Polo, Marco, 86-87, *89*

Portugal, 90, 95, 99, 138, 149; exploration and colonies of, 90, 95, 99, 112, 136, 138

Presley, Elvis, 171

R

Racism, 141, 154, 169-71

Rapa Nui (Easter Island), 8, 9

Religions: Buddhism, 56, 57, 60, 136; Confucianism, 37, 57, 60, 119; Jainism, 55, 136; Parsee, 55, 136; Shinto, 56; Sikhism, 55, 167, 183; Taoism, 57, 60; *see also entries for* Christianity, Hinduism, Islam, Judaism

188

Richthofen, Manfred von (Red Baron), 150

Roman Empire, 58, 59, 64, 66, 69-75, 77-78, 80, 83-85, 115, 134; and idea of the "republic," 71, 74, 80, 108, 109, 130; and persecution of Christians, 59, 73

Roosevelt, Franklin, 161, 162

Russia, 7, 9, 11, 30, 112, *133*, 141, 148, 149, 155-57, 158, 160, 162, 163, 166, 174, 177; Russian Revolution, 156-57; *see also* Soviet Union

S

Saladin (Salah ad-Din), 82

Scandinavia, 11, 79, 84, 89

Scotland, 107, 118, 177

Scythians, 21, 29-30, 101

Serbia, 148

Shi Huangdi (Qin), Emperor (China), 35-39, 42, 86

Siberia, 7, 156, 157, 158

Sitting Bull, 146

Slavery, 42, 104-105, 108, 112, 117, 130, 135, 139, 141, 142, 145, 156, 169

Smith, Adam, 129

Socialism, 130, 157

South Africa, 153, 154, 170-71; apartheid in, 170-71

Soviet Union, 157-58, 162, 166, 173-74, 178; Communist Party of, 157; *see also* Russia

Space travel, 178-79

Spain, 9, 10, 59, 70, 71, 74, 81, 84, 90, 96, 105-108, 112, 176; and the Armada, 105-106; and the Conquistadors, 96-98, 99, 103, 106, 108; exploration and colonies of, 93-99, 105-108, 112

Stalin, Joseph, 157-58, 160, 162, 166, 174

Stanley, Henry, 135

Sumeria, 39-43, 50, 53

T

Tasmania, 6, 11

Tibet, 56, 60

Tokugawa family (Japan), 139, 140

Totalitarianism, 158

Trading, 18-19, 24, 29, 31, 41, 42, 45, 46, 50, 66, 74, 84-85, 89, 90, 95, 100, 102-103, 116-17, 119, 120, 136, 140; and the Silk Road, 86, 87

Turkey, 19, 64, 66, 74

U

Ukraine, 6, 29, 79, 158, 165, 174

Union of Soviet Socialist Republics, *see* Russia; Soviet Union

United Nations, 165, 166, 168-69

United States, 19, 100, 102, 103, 109, 112, 117, 123, 124, 125, 127, 139, 140, 141-47, 150, 151, 159, 160-61, 162, 164, 165, 166, 173; and American Revolution, 108-109; and Civil War, 141-45, 146, 169; immigration to, 145, 147; industrialization in, 121, 122, 124, 128, 143; racism in, 169-70; slavery in, 104; and war with native peoples, 145-46

V

Victoria, Queen (England), *133*, 133-34, 137, 138, 147, 173

Vietnam, 51; Cham people of, 51; Vietnam War, 173

Vikings, 89, 90

W

Washington, George, 109

Watt, James, 116

West Indies, 103, 104, 139

Wilhelm II, Kaiser (Germany), 147, 158

Wilson, Woodrow, 151

World War One, 147-51, *153*, 155, 158, 160, 161, 173

World War Two, 161-63, 167, 172, 183

Wright, Orville and Wilbur, 150

X

Xerxes, King (Persia), 68

Z

Zheng He, 88-89, *89*

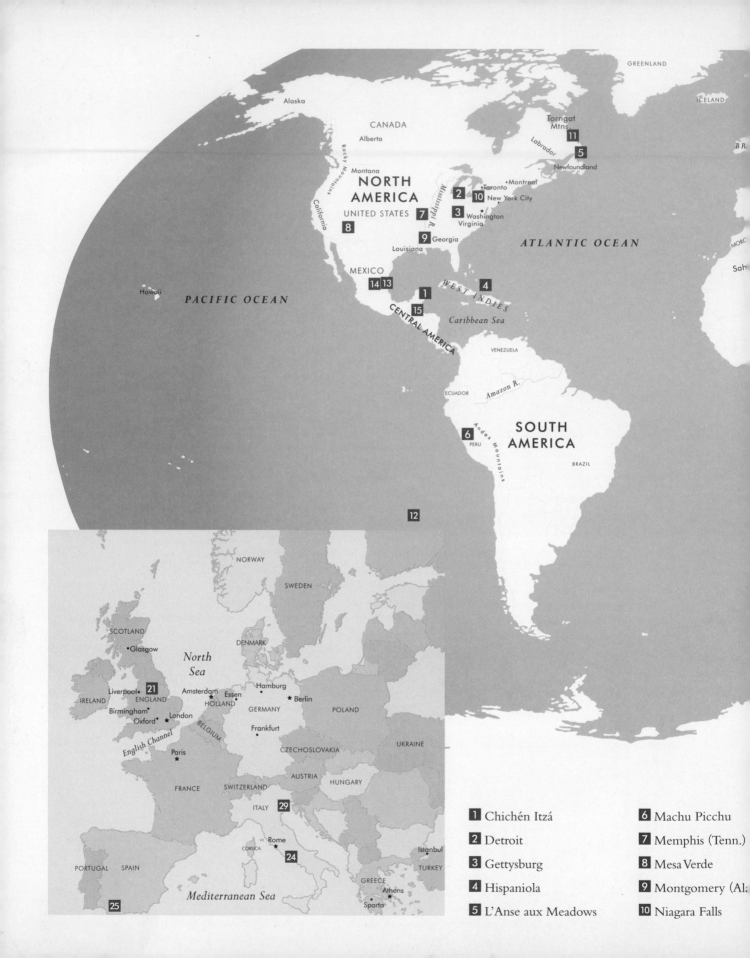

GREENLAND

ICELAND

Alaska

CANADA

Alberta

Torngat Mtns. **11**

Labrador

5 Newfoundland

BR

Montana

Rocky Mountains

Mississippi R.

NORTH AMERICA

2 Toronto • Montreal

10 New York City

UNITED STATES **7**

3 Washington

Virginia

ATLANTIC OCEAN

California

8

9 Georgia

Louisiana

MOR

Sah

Hawaii

PACIFIC OCEAN

MEXICO

14 **13**

1

WEST INDIES

4

15

Caribbean Sea

CENTRAL AMERICA

VENEZUELA

ECUADOR

Amazon R.

SOUTH AMERICA

Andes Mountains

6

PERU

BRAZIL

12

NORWAY

SWEDEN

SCOTLAND

• Glasgow

North Sea

DENMARK

Hamburg •

IRELAND

Liverpool •

21

ENGLAND

Amsterdam ★

Essen

★ Berlin

GERMANY

POLAND

Birmingham •

Oxford •

London ★

HOLLAND

BELGIUM

Frankfurt •

UKRAINE

English Channel

Paris ★

CZECHOSLOVAKIA

FRANCE

SWITZERLAND

AUSTRIA

HUNGARY

ITALY

29

PORTUGAL

SPAIN

Rome ★

CORSICA

24

Istanbul •

TURKEY

GREECE

Athens ★

Sparta •

Mediterranean Sea

25

1 Chichén Itzá	**6** Machu Picchu
2 Detroit	**7** Memphis (Tenn.)
3 Gettysburg	**8** Mesa Verde
4 Hispaniola	**9** Montgomery (Ala
5 L'Anse aux Meadows	**10** Niagara Falls